TERRIFIC T-SHIRTS

TERRIFIC T-SHIRTS

Hundreds of Ways to Create Your Own Great Designs

Chris Rankin

LARK BOOKS

A Division of Sterling Publishing Co., Inc.

New York

Editor: Chris Rankin
Art Director: Shannon Yokeley
Photographers: Richard Babb and Evan Bracken
Cover Designer: Barbara Zaretsky
Illustrators: Chris Colando, Scott Lowrey, and Lance Wille
Editorial Assistance: Delores Gosnell

Library of Congress Cataloging-in-Publication Data

Rankin, Chris.
  Terrific t-shirts : hundreds of ways to create your own
great designs / by Chris Rankin.– 1st ed.
        p. cm.
Includes index.
   ISBN 1-57990-574-9 (pbk.)
   1. Textile painting. 2. T-shirts. 3. Stencil work. 4. Textile
printing. I. Title.
TT851.R36 2004
746.6–dc22

                                        2003022533

10 9 8 7 6 5 4 3 2 1

First Edition

Published by Lark Books, a division of
Sterling Publishing Co., Inc.
387 Park Avenue South, New York, N.Y. 10016

© 2004, Lark Books

Distributed in Canada by Sterling Publishing
c/o Canadian Manda Group, One Atlantic Ave., Suite 105
Toronto, Ontario, Canada M6K 3E7

Distributed in the U.K. by Guild of Master Craftsman Publications Ltd.
Castle Place, 166 High Street, Lewes, East Sussex, England BN7 1XU
Tel: (+ 44) 1273 477374, Fax: (+ 44) 1273 478606
Email: pubs@thegmcgroup.com, Web: www.gmcpublications.com

Distributed in Australia by Capricorn Link (Australia) Pty Ltd.
P.O. Box 704, Windsor, NSW 2756 Australia

If you have questions or comments about this book, please contact:
Lark Books
67 Broadway
Asheville, NC 28801
(828) 253-0467

Manufactured in China

1-57990-574-9

Contents

Introduction

It seems like a long, long time ago that T-shirts meant underwear. For most of us, they have become a clothing essential and a reflection of who we are. Luckily, unlike other wardrobe necessities, T-shirts are cheap enough to purchase by the dozen. You probably have casual T's for wearing to the grocery store; well-worn favorites for sleeping in; tattered-but-cherished friends perfect for cleaning the house in; shirts in this season's colors to accessorize office attire; and designer styles that announce that you know what's in and what's out. Some of your T's are likely solid colors, others probably have some type of surface design, and some may even broadcast your political and cultural allegiances—namely, I sent you money and all I got was this, well, wonderful T-shirt!

If the only gap in your T-shirt wardrobe is in the category of "I made this myself," here's your chance to change that—and have a ball doing it. A plain, white T makes an ideal blank canvas; for very little money and very little personal risk, you can express yourself in an amazing number of ways with color, line, and texture. The talented designers who created shirts for this book had a lot of fun in the process. Some of them are professional T-shirt makers, others are well-known surface designers, and most are artists or designers in another field. What they share is an enthusiasm for expressing a design idea on a T-shirt. So many products are now available for adding color and design to fabric, that the designers' biggest challenge was deciding whether to paint, embellish, tie-dye, bleach, batik, stamp, marble, screenprint, or use a photo transfer. I am delighted with the result of their choices, and I hope you will be, too.

The book features more than 150 distinctive and inspirational designs that transform a plain T-shirt, using a variety of materials and techniques. The shirts are organized into sections according to these different surface design methods, and in each section you'll find basic information for working with that technique or material. There are many excellent books devoted to a single subject, such as screenprinting. If a particular method wins your heart, I encourage you to read more about it.

Feel free to make one or more of the shirts in the book, or use them as jumping off points for your own designs. You may want to experiment first on a piece of an old 100-percent cotton bed sheet. Look around you for design motifs—the world is full of them. Leaves covered with paint make perfect stamps; line drawings in books can be copied on clear acetate or tracing paper; and favorite black-and-white photos can be the starting point for screened images. You may feel drawn to bind a shirt with rope and immerse it in dye as soon as possible. Or you may feel compelled to drizzle hot wax on a shirt with an interesting tool called a tjanting. Or your way may be to mix a palette of paints you like, wet a brush, take a deep breath, and give Matisse a run for his money.

Depending on how your very own terrific T-shirt turns out, you can decide whether to sleep in it or wear it to your next social gathering. Then again, you can always try again. And again. Just for the fun of it.

Ready, Set, Go!

Selecting a T-Shirt

Undecorated T-shirts are blank canvases just waiting to be transformed with color and design. And they are everywhere: most discount, department, outlet, and fashion stores carry T-shirts at reasonable prices. Today's T's feature a variety of necklines, such as your basic crew, v, and boat. Some are cropped at the waist, others are tunic length, and most are what you would call regular. T-shirts sport a range of sleeve styles—short, long, elbow length, flared, cuffed, or not there at all. Fabric weights range from beefy to silky. And although plain white is still a classic, you can find T-shirts in every imaginable color. T's are available for large and small adults, for children of all ages, and for babies, too. There is a lot to choose from.

Take your pick, based on your budget, personal preference, and the other criteria listed below.

1. Most of the fabric paints and dyes discussed in this book deliver the truest and most long-lasting color on 100 percent cotton. A few work best on synthetics, and some do fine on 50:50 cotton/synthetic blends. Always read the manufacturer's suggestions concerning the most appropriate fabric for the application you want to use.

2. Most techniques require that you wash the shirt at least twice during the process, and many involve setting the color with heat. Even T's that claim to be preshrunk may get a wee bit smaller under these conditions. So it's a good idea to buy a size that will fit you or a friend after a few forays in the washer and dryer.

3. In general, a heavyweight T-shirt will have a longer life span and will hold the design better than a flimsy one.

4. For most designs, you will probably want to avoid a T-shirt with a pocket.

5. Although a white T-shirt is certainly the most flexible and inviting blank canvas for your creativity, you can do some interesting designs on a colored shirt. Discharge dying, for instance, where you bleach the color out of a shirt to achieve certain effects, demands a colored shirt. Some designs are going to look best on basic black. Or you may prefer a colored background for a particular motif and don't want to dye the shirt when you can buy one in that color. It's important, however, to be aware that most fabric paints and dyes are transparent, which means that the color of the fabric will bleed through the paint and affect its color.

Ready, Set, Go!

Understanding Your Tools and Materials

Experienced artists and crafters know the importance of being familiar with the tools and supplies they use to create particular effects. With so many products available for decorating fabric, it can be a challenge to know about all of them and to be sure you are using the right one for the look you want to achieve.

1. Visit your local craft-supply store, and, if you have one in your area, a good artist-supply store. Be prepared to stay awhile: you may be astonished and bewildered by all the choices. Salespeople usually have a wealth of information about the products and techniques the store offers, and can help you determine what will best accomplish your design needs. Some of these stores offer classes on particular techniques and products.

2. Read the product directions carefully in the store and again when you are ready to work on your T-shirt. Manufacturers have a vested interest in making sure you know how to use their products and in helping to ensure you are satisfied with the results so you will purchase those items more than once.

3. Use mail-order art-supply catalogs to learn about hard-to-find products and tools. Some catalogs specialize in items specifically for surface design, and they are very informative.

Getting Ready

1. Wash and dry the T-shirt to remove the sizing the manufacturer has probably added. Don't skip this step: sizing prevents paint and dyes from working the way they should. Do not use fabric softener.

2. Iron the shirt so that your canvas starts out without wrinkles. If you choose to wear the finished shirt with plenty of wrinkles, that's your business!

3. Prepare an appropriate work surface. This can be set up on your kitchen table or in a corner of a family room. Surface design can be messy, so be sure your work area is protected from paint drips or the damage resulting from sharp cutting tools.

4. Devise a method of preventing the paint or dye from bleeding through the front of the shirt and winding up in splotches on the back. You can simply insert something inside the shirt—a few layers of newspaper or rags, or a piece of cardboard with waxed paper taped over it.

If you are going to paint the shirt, stretch the fabric so it's taut but not pulled out of shape. You don't want your moving brush to scrunch up the fabric and skip over a wrinkle. You may want to tape the shirt to your work surface with masking tape or pin it down with tacks.

If you are going to stamp or screen print the shirt, you need a firm, lightly padded surface. Cut a piece of cardboard or foam core to fit inside the shirt, cover it with a layer of batting or a double thickness of fabric, and cover that with waxed paper.

You can also purchase, for not much money, pieces of cardboard shaped like T-shirts that stretch the fabric and protect the back. These forms, available at most discount and craft-supply stores, are very useful when you need the entire shirt to be held rigid. It is still a good idea to cover these forms with waxed paper.

Batik and marbling require different preparations and are discussed on pages 125 and 151.

5. Unless you are planning to cover the entire T-shirt with an overall application of dye—for instance, by tie-dying or marbling the fabric—you may want to mark the center of the shirt so that you can plan the placement of your design. Then try the shirt on or ask a friend to do so, and mark where you want the designed area to wind up so it looks good when a person is inside. That way you can be sure that the designed area will fall, let's say, on the chest area and not on the tummy, unless that is where you want the design to be. Mark the design area with chalk or ordinary pencil. Or you can use fabric markers with disappearing ink: the marks will fade away when the shirt is washed.

Painting & Embellishing

Many varieties of paint, markers, crayons, pastel sticks, and dyes are specially formulated for use on fabric, and there are many types of tools for applying them.

NOTE: No matter what kind of material or technique you use to apply color to the shirt, always insert a piece of clean cardboard or other sturdy paper inside the shirt to prevent the paint or dye from bleeding through the front of the shirt and coloring the back, unless that is the effect you want.

MATERIALS

Fabric Paints

Also called textile paints, fabric paints are remarkably easy to use and can create many different effects. The simplest way to apply fabric paints is with a brush. The paint becomes light- and wash-fast after you heat set the painted T-shirt by ironing it on the wrong side or by putting it in the clothes dryer. The manufacturer's instructions will suggest the best way to heat-set the product. If you skip this step, the fabric paint will wash out the first time you wash the shirt. Some designers suggest that you wait a week before washing the shirt to let the paint set into the fabric. If you're painting on a brand-new shirt, you might also want to wash the T-shirt before you begin to remove any sizing that could interfere with the fabric paint.

Textile paints come in bright as well as subdued colors that stay strong through repeated washings. They are available in a wide range of formulations, including metallic, opaque, pearlescent, fluorescent, iridescent, and glitter. Most of the paints designed for silk will work on cotton, as well: they flow easily across the fabric and create a watercolor effect.

Fabric Markers

Fabric markers come in an astonishing array of colors. Using a fine, medium, or wide tip, you can draw images, lines, or words, or add shading and detail to a design. Other kinds of pens and markers can be used to decorate a T-shirt, as long as they are described as indelible on fabric.

*This gorgeous shirt, left, was hand-painted by **Amanda Kibler** to represent the color palette she used one year for much of her surface design work. She mixed textile inks to achieve the desired colors. Then she applied them to a laundered, 100 percent cotton shirt, using foam brushes, a small ruler, and her fingers. When the ink was dry, she used a fine-tipped brush and black ink to write in the names and numbers of each color. This is one artist palette you can proudly leave the studio wearing!*

Painting & Embellishing

Dimensional Paints

Known to many kids and crafters as "puff" paints, these child-friendly paints are worth considering because they are fun to use and because—if applied with planning and restraint—they can add attractive detail and texture to a design. Squeeze out the dimensional paint carefully from its plastic applicator bottle to create a thin line of color that dries permanently. Use it to outline shapes, write words and numbers, and accent colors.

Fabric Transfer Crayons

Fabric transfer crayons, sometimes called paint crayons, are as much fun to use as the ordinary children's crayons they resemble. Sketch a design on white paper and color it to your liking. Place the paper, colored side down, on the T-shirt, and iron over the back of the paper. The heat transfers the color to the shirt. These crayons are best suited to synthetic fabrics, although they will work on 50:50 cotton/poly blends.

Pastel Dye Sticks

Unlike the artists' pastels they resemble, these pastels are made to be used on fabric, but the finished effect is remarkably similar to that of regular pastels. For best results, use them on natural fibers, although they will work on cotton/poly blends, too. Draw and color directly on the shirt, blending and overlapping colors. Heat-set the colors with an iron, as described in the manufacturer's directions.

Fiber Reactive Dyes

Most often used to dye a piece of fabric by immersing it in a dye bath, fiber reactive dyes, often called fabric dyes, can also be applied with a brush to "paint" color onto an area of a shirt to create a random pattern or a specific design. The advantage of working with these dyes is that they do not stiffen the fabric. Paint, even high-quality fabric paint, sits on the surface of the fabric, thereby changing the feel or "hand" of the fabric, making it a bit stiffer and heavier. Dyes, however, chemically react with the fibers to become part of the fabric, so a dyed shirt feels just as soft as it did before the dye was applied.

If you plan to apply fabric dye to only certain areas of your T-shirt, you will need to thicken it with sodium alginate, a harmless seaweed extract available where you purchase fabric dyes. This powdered extract prevents dye from bleeding across the fabric where you do not want it. Sprinkle some into a small amount of water in a blender, whirl the mixture for a few seconds, and then add the dye to the resulting gel.

Some fiber-reactive dye colors break down into their component colors, which creates a rim of color around each stroke. Two of Sandra Holzman's shirts (pages 36 and 37) are based on loose, well spaced strokes of dye and their rims of different color. First, Holzman washed and prepped the white shirts as described on page 36. Then she applied the dyes with large brushes, letting the dye soak through the front and back so that the two sides are identical. She left space between the strokes so that the dye could bleed, creating attractive and surprising effects.

Added Flair

The lure of any good craft or fabric store is that it has aisles bursting with beads, buttons, ribbons, sequins, fringe, trim, iron-on patches, and countless other colorful ornaments. If you've always wished you had more ways to put these irresistible adornments to use, embellished T-shirts offer an answer. Choose lightweight and smallish pieces rather than heavy, dangling ones. They're perfect for one-of-a-kind accents that don't cause T-shirts to stretch or sag.

Miscellaneous

Plastic syringes and plastic squeeze bottles with narrow tips are very useful for applying a very fine line of paint, dye, or bleach onto the shirt. Both are available where dyes and paints are sold.

TECHNIQUES

Brushing

Stock up on a good supply of ordinary paintbrushes in various sizes: narrow for applying fine lines of fabric paint, broad for covering larger areas. Bristles that are somewhat stiff, such as those made of nylon, effectively force paint down inside the fabric weave. Foam brushes sold at hardware and craft-supply shops are handy for applying paint to achieve a range of effects. Use an inexpensive brush to apply bleach to a T-shirt; the bleach will, in no time, destroy the bristles.

Rolling

Small foam or napped rollers designed for house painting can be used to paint T-shirts. One simple approach is to cover the roller surface with bands of different colors of paint, and then roll the paint onto the shirt from one shoulder down to the opposite hem or straight across the middle of the shirt.

Stenciling

Stencils are easy to make and allow you to effectively block paint out of certain areas and direct it to other areas to form a design. You can use a number of materials as stencils, as long as they will cut easily and repel paint; heavy-stock paper, cardboard, clear acetate, or waxed stenciling paper all work well. Or you can use materials that will stick to the shirt, such as masking tape and contact shelf paper. You can also use freezer paper: Cut your stencil, place it shiny-side-down onto the shirt, and iron on the freezer paper.

Look around you for other objects that could become stencils—all they need is holes or an interesting shape. A paper doily, the punched perforated edges of computer paper, a piece of chair caning, the brim of an old straw hat, a fly swatter, and a string shopping bag would all block out interesting patterns.

To achieve the best results, use a stubby stenciling brush or a foam brush and a small amount of paint. Rather than stroking the brush back and forth, dab the paint into the cutout areas, using a gentle up-and-down motion.

Try using bleach instead of paint. Attach the stencil to the shirt, fill a spray bottle with diluted bleach, and spray. All the cutout areas will turn pale. When the shirt has discharged the desired amount of color, quickly immerse it in a neutralizing solution.

Sponging

You can create a variety of looks by applying paint to a T-shirt with an ordinary household sponge. You can add a complementary color and a hint of texture on top of an area of the shirt you have already painted, as is done often on painted walls, or you can sponge small dabs of color onto an unpainted shirt.

Pour a small amount of fabric paint into a disposable pie pan or plastic foam tray, and use a small spatula to spread out the paint. Dip the sponge (trim it first to the size you want) in the paint and dab it on the shirt. You may want to practice this technique on a scrap of fabric first. That way you will know how much paint to apply to the sponge to create the look you want. You can also cut several large sponges into a variety of shapes, and use them to create the effect of stamping. (See Ellen Zahorec's flower shirt on page 41).

Daubing

You can imitate the look of airbrushing by daubing on the paint. A dauber leaves a thin layer of paint and interesting color gradations. To make one, wad up a piece of thin foam rubber, wrap another piece of foam around it, and secure the neck with a rubber band. Pour a small amount of paint into a flat container, and work the dauber into it so the paint penetrates the foam layers. Then, with a patting motion, daub the paint onto the shirt.

Discharge Dyeing

One popular method of creating a design on a T-shirt is to remove the color from a colored shirt using diluted chlorine bleach. Discharge dying can yield surprising and pleasing results.

To paint away color, make a diluted solution—one part liquid household bleach to three parts tap water—and apply it to the shirt with an old brush. You can also make a discharge paste using thiourea dioxide, soda ash, liquid detergent, and water, and applying it with a plastic squeeze bottle. (Experiment with these bleach solutions on fabric scraps. Try to use the least possible amount of bleach to achieve the desired shade.) It is best to work outdoors or in a very well ventilated area when using discharge solutions, as the fumes are irritating and, in large quantities, can be toxic.

When the shirt has discharged as much color as you want, plunge it immediately into a neutralizing solution: either $\frac{1}{4}$ cup (59 ml) vinegar to 1 quart (946 ml) water, or 1 tablespoon (4.9 ml) sodium bisulfite to 1 quart (946 ml) water.

You can also achieve attractive results (and discharge a bad mood!) by spattering or outright throwing undiluted bleach directly onto the shirt. (This approach may give you the confidence to throw paint at a canvas!) This technique is best done outdoors. Neutralize the shirt as described above or rinse it in cold water and then promptly wash it in a small amount of laundry soap.

Embellishing

There are two main ways to add embellishments such as beads and fringe. One is to stitch them in place. Sew beads on much the same way you'd sew a button on a shirt. Thread your needle with standard, color-coordinated thread, knot the two ends of thread together, bring the needle from the inside of the shirt up through the bead's hole and back down. Repeat the process four or five times. For added strength, poke the needle back up through the shirt a final time but don't go through the bead, wrap around the threads twice, then bring the needle back to the inside of the shirt, and tie off the knot. To sew on ribbons, fringe, pieces of fabric, and similar items, first "baste" the embellishment in place with a few dots of fabric glue or hold it in position with straight pins, then use a basic running stitch. Thread your needle, make a knot on one end of the thread, drive the needle up from the inside of the shirt, and insert it through the embellishment and

the shirt several times at evenly spaced intervals. Pull the needle and thread through, and repeat. Or, if you have a sewing machine, by all means, use it.

If you want to skip working with a needle altogether, use fabric glue or fusible web to attach your embellishment. Be sure to read the manufacturer's suggested uses before you start. Fabric glue is simple but slightly less durable, and it can make some materials stiff. For a stronger solution, use fusible web. When placed between two pieces of fabric and ironed, this white, mesh-like material melts and bonds to the pieces. You can buy fusible web in rolls $\frac{1}{2}$ inch (1.3 cm) thick. Iron-on patches come with a fusible-web backing already in place.

Painting & Embellishing

Liz Hughey had fun painting glittery fantasy flowers on a blue tank-style T-shirt. First she sketched the flowers with white chalk. Then she painted in the petals, stems, and leaves with red, blue, and green fabric paint in a gloss finish. To give the flowers more texture, she squeezed the paint onto the design area from the squeeze bottle, and then used a brush to spread the paint. When dry, she painted in the gold petals with metallic paint, then accented them with red centers. Finally, she used red and blue dimensional paint to outline the petals and add detail to the blue centers of the flowers.

Betty Kershner painted with dyes to give a soft hand to the finished shirt and the effect of a watercolor. First she put a white, 100 percent cotton shirt on a T-shirt board and painted the front with sodium alginate to prevent the dye from bleeding across the fabric. She let the shirt dry and painted the design with fiber reactive dyes, using a fan brush and foam brushes. She let the shirt dry again and then waited 24 hours before washing it in hot water.

Painting & Embellishing

You can almost see the scales on this cheerful lizard. Designer **Marcia Winters** first sketched her design on a piece of paper, playing with shapes and colors until she liked what she saw. Then she pinned a white shirt to a board, so that it was taut but not stretched out of shape, and outlined the design on the shirt itself, using a soft lead pencil. She thinned some fabric paints with a little textile medium and, using a round brush, painted one color at a time in a rhythmic back-and-forth motion.

Dana Irwin combined a couple of well-placed accents with a festive homemade stencil and vibrant colors to create a shirt that shouts ole! First, she traced an image of two dancers onto several pieces of thin cardstock. She settled on her color combination, and used a craft knife to cut out one stencil for each color. With a textile brush, she applied textile dye one color at a time, working carefully so she wouldn't blur past the stencil edges. She continued to apply dye until she achieved the color density she wanted, then followed the dye packaging instructions to fix it. For a few finishing splashes, she sewed on faux-pearl buttons as spats and a silk-rose hair bauble.

Painting & Embellishing

Jean Penland created this tiny T and the one on page (197) for her grandsons, Luke and Matthew. Here she cut stencils for the birds. Then she filled in the designs with fabric paint and markers, leaving plenty of white space for the birds to flap around in. When the paint was dry, she ironed the shirt on the wrong side to set the paints.

To make this happy shirt, **Ellen Zahorec** started by coloring four strips of paper with fabric crayons (press hard when you color and fill in the strips as densely as you can). She accordion-folded the strips and cut out simple paper dolls. She saved the scraps of paper to use as design elements.

She covered her ironing board with a thick layer of newspaper and ironed the paper flat. Then she placed the shirt on the ironing board and slipped newspaper inside the shirt. She arranged the cut-paper dolls and the scraps of paper, colored side down, on the shirt and covered them with a piece of clean newspaper. She then ironed the shirt on a high setting for about three minutes, moving the iron slowly and evenly to ensure even heat and to avoid shifting the drawings. (You can peek under an edge of a drawing to see if the color is visible yet.) When the crayons transferred to the shirt, she removed the paper. As a last touch, Zahorec added details and highlights using dry-erase markers.

Painting & Embellishing

Craft and fabric stores carry a wide variety of iron-on appliqués that show off the hottest styles of the season, as well as more classic motifs. Nothing could be easier than selecting some that suit your fancy and affixing multiples to a T-shirt. That's what **Terry Taylor** did with the mother-daughter set shown here and on the facing page. He simply followed the instructions on the appliqué packaging for covering the embellishments with a protective cloth and pressing them in place with an iron. For the adult version of the pair, he chose two green flower designs and scattered them across the front and sleeves of a yellow shirt.

To make a child's shirt to coordinate with the one on the facing page, **Terry Taylor** chose smaller flowers in a complementary color, plus dragonflies and a butterfly, and ironed them on in a sweet little semicircle around the shirt's neck. Be sure to read the manufacturer's recommendations for laundering before purchasing any appliqués. You want those that can withstand at least delicate washing.

Painting & Embellishing

If you're into Mexican food, you might as well get really into it; paint some bright red chili peppers on your shirt. **Peggy DeBell** cut a pepper shaped paper stencil and, using a medium brush, applied red fabric paint inside the cut-out (or negative) shapes. She used fabric markers to outline the peppers, color the stems, and draw the vines. For the background, she brushed fabric paint on a large household sponge and stamped it repeatedly on the shirt.

Why is it, **Layne Goldsmith's** husband inquired, that there's camouflage clothing for desert and jungle, but none for the place you really need to hide—the city?

Goldsmith set to work.

She cut brick shapes from self-adhesive shelf paper, peeled off the backing, and stuck the bricks onto a maroon T-shirt. Then, using stiff nylon brushes, she painted a "mortar" of gray and white fabric paint between the bricks. After the mortar was dry, she removed the bricks, heat-set the paint, and handed the shirt to her husband. There you go, she said. Urban camouflage.

Painting & Embellishing

Polka dots are one of the best-loved design motifs ever. **Allison Smith's** bold, bright shirt shows why—they make for a downright happy look. She used photo-reactive paint, washers and coins, and a steady stream of direct sunlight to create the shirt. After inserting a cardboard form inside the shirt, she spread everything out on a taped-down plastic drop cloth outside. She diluted red photo-reactive paint with water in one plastic container and yellow in another, according to the paint's packaging directions, then filled a third plastic container with plain water. With a sponge paintbrush, she wet the shirt thoroughly with water. Working quickly, she painted three or four long red "S" lines on the shirt, then painted in between the red lines with yellow, and blended the yellow paint into the red to create color variations of orange. Immediately after painting, she placed the washers and coins on the shirt in a random pattern, and let everything sit undisturbed in the sun until the pattern developed. This typically takes 15 minutes to one hour.

Know someone young at heart who might like to shake things up with a new shirt? **Terry Taylor** has designed just the one. To make this kicky cropped version, he started with a standard shirt and marked the crop line with a pin, then laid it flat, eyeballed an extra $5/8$ inch (1.6 cm) margin for a hem, and cut through both layers of the shirt. He turned up the raw edge and hemmed it with iron-on fusible web tape. You could also stitch the hem by hand or machine. He laid the shirt flat again, measured its width, then, just to be on the safe side, doubled that measurement and added 6 inches (15.2 cm). He used the measurement to figure out how much ball fringe he needed. He stitched the fringe in place from the inside of the hem, so it would stand up to regular laundering.

Painting & Embellishing

Create a spring garden with simple-to-use fabric markers. That's exactly what **Liz Hughey** did—with glorious results. You don't have to press hard to get good color with these markers, you can vary the weight of the line, and they dry permanently after only 24 hours. Hughey sketched a design on paper first, then plunged in and painted the flowers freehand on the shirt, using a selection of markers in bright colors.

S helley Lowell had fun sponging fabric paint in bright colors onto a purple shirt to create this simple diagonal pattern. She bought a package of uninflated sponges (dry and flat) in a craft-supply store. With a craft knife she cut out little bars from the flat sponge and then wet the cut pieces so they would inflate. She let them dry overnight. She put on the shirt and used masking tape to indicate where she wanted to print. Then she placed the shirt on a flat surface. Lowell spread five colors of fabric paint on paper plates and used separate sponges to print the stripes. Finally, she sewed on buttons, including two that hold up the cuffs.

Painting & Embellishing

Terry Taylor put a store-bought paper doily to use as a T-shirt stencil and had terrific results. He started by choosing a doily shape that suited him. Then he sprayed each side with acrylic spray to strengthen it and make it less likely to tear. He laid his shirt on a flat surface and, once the doily was dry, sprayed the back side of the doily with a light coat of aerosol glue, positioned it in the center of the shirt, and smoothed it in place. He then slid a layer of paper between the front and back of the shirt to protect the back from the fabric paint. With a dry stencil brush, he pounced black paint through the stencil, then neatened the shape's edge with a small brush. He let the paint dry thoroughly before peeling off the doily, and finished by setting the fabric paint according to its packaging instructions.

To make this sweet band of hearts along the bottom of a pink shirt, **Terry Taylor** prepared several small, heart-shaped doilies to serve as stencils, following the same process described on page 30. He positioned the doilies along the bottom edge of the shirt, securing them with a light coat of aerosol glue, and slid a layer of paper between the front and back of the shirt to protect the back from the fabric paint. With masking tape, he marked off the top and bottom of a border around the band of hearts. Using a dry stencil brush, he pounced gold metallic paint through the heart stencils, being careful not to overwork them, then filled in the taped-off border area. He let the paint dry thoroughly before peeling off the doilies, and finished by setting the fabric paint according to its packaging instructions.

Painting & Embellishing

On this olive shirt **Lenore Davis** used a technique called "frottage"—essentially a rubbing of a raised, textured surface. To create a frottage surface, she soaked a piece of heavy, absorbent paper in water, then hand-folded and twisted it. She laid it between layers of newspaper, covered it with a board, and weighted it down. After a few hours she removed it from the press and allowed it to get almost dry, then pressed it again to flatten it. Finally, she inserted the wrinkled paper inside the shirt.

To apply the paint she made a "dauber"—soft foam wadded into a ball (see page 14)—and spread a small amount of black textile paint on a Styrofoam tray. She dipped the dauber in the paint and applied it to the shirt sparingly, using a patting, up-and-down motion, moving the wrinkled paper around as necessary. After the black paint was dry she repeated the process, this time with iridescent orange.

Huge, brilliant, almost comic in their extravagance, sunflowers triumph over good sense. **Marilyn Forth** captured some of that spirit on a T-shirt. She sketched flowers and leaves on paper, then traced them onto the shirt. Working with pastel dye sticks, she layered color upon color directly on the shirt, for a painterly effect.

Painting & Embellishing

If you can loop thread or yarn around a needle a few times, you know everything you need to about creating one of embroidery's easiest and most charming stitches: the French knot.

Lynne Caldwell used it to dot a delightful band of knots along the bottom edge of a shirt and a neat row around each sleeve. She used two shades of small-gauge rayon yarn—green and gold. To create the band, she knotted green on an embroidery needle, anchored the yarn on the back side of the shirt, brought the needle through to the front, looped the yarn a few times to create a knot, then inserted the needle back through the shirt. She repeated this process until she had enough green knots, then switched to gold. She used the same technique with gold yarn to create an even row of knots around each sleeve. To finish the neck of the shirt, she used a standard running stitch. First, she used green yarn. Then she offset a second set of running stitches in gold.

In addition to providing an enchanting accent all by themselves, French knots, discovered **Lynne Caldwell**, can frolic quite nicely with beads. To decorate the V-neck of this powder-blue shirt, she scattered a combination of the embroidered knots (see page 34 for how to create them) and tiny, translucent blue beads. She attached the beads with the same yarn she used for the knots, sewing each in place just as you would a button. Below the neck, she used a second simple embroidery stitch—a whipstitch— to create three slender stems. To whipstitch, simply make tiny, even, slanted stitches. She topped off one stem with French knots in the shape a flower head and added beads to the base of two stems.

Painting & Embellishing

Sandra Holzman achieved beautiful, water-color looking results by painting dye onto a wet 100 percent cotton T-shirt. First she placed the shirt on a covered work surface, smoothing out all wrinkles. With a large brush (2 to 3 inches wide [5 to 7.5 cm]), she applied fiber reactive dyes. She did not put cardboard inside the shirt because she wanted the dye to soak through the front of the shirt and color the back with the same pattern. The key to these shirts is that Holzman deliberately left space between each swath of dye to leave room for the dye to bleed. Some dye colors break down along the edges into their component parts, which leaves a rim of color around each stroke of dye. This process may take as long as 30 minutes to occur. Holzman waited patiently to see how each dye bled before applying the next color to complement the rim color.

This lovely bleached and dyed shirt was created by **Sandra Holzman** using the approach described on page 36. After brushing on the dye and allowing the color to bleed, Holzman applied discharge paste with a squeeze bottle to remove color and create patterns that complement the way in which the dye bled. The color is removed from the shirt, but not all the way back to the original white, so a new color appeared. Then she applied another layer of color by sponging on textile dyes. To accent the dye and discharge patterns, Holzman dipped a seed-potato net bag in silver metallic paint, and then smacked the bag on the shirt, front and back.

Painting & Embellishing

To create a canvas, **Chris Colando** brushed a bleach solution on the front of a black T-shirt. (Use a cheap brush, he advises; the bleach eats it up fast.) With a beige rectangle to work on, Colando applied broad strokes of black and white fabric paints to create a striking abstract design.

Once a canvas is bleached in the middle of a shirt, virtually anything can be painted on it. **Chris Colando** used black and white fabric paints to create a landscape, complete with hills, shrubs, and trees.

Painting & Embellishing

Fabric transfer crayons provided the vibrant colors for these animal cutouts. **Ellen Zahorec** crayoned white sheets of paper in various colors—one color per sheet—then cut animal shapes out of the bright papers. She laid each pattern color-side-down on a white shirt and ironed it on the back to transfer the color, overlapping designs until the zoo was full.

Simple sponging with bright colors can make a garden bloom on a shirt like this one designed by **Ellen Zahorec**. She cut cellulose sponges into the shapes of flowers and leaves. She evenly spread a small amount of textile ink on a paper plate and gently patted the sponge in the paint about 10 times to ensure even distribution of the ink on the sponge. She inserted a clean piece of newspaper inside the shirt and laid the shirt on a flat surface. Then she gently patted the sponge on the shirt. For a textured effect she patted only once; more pressure with the sponge gives a more solid look. She repeated this process with all the colors and shapes, overlapping the designs to create the impression of depth. Finally, she used the edge of a piece of cardboard to paint the grass and stems.

Painting & Embellishing

Friendly fish swim across this child-size shirt, perhaps on their way to freedom in a child-size swimming pool. Designer **Liz Hughey** used a fish stencil and pastel dye sticks. First she cut the fish stencil. Then she applied a layer of pastel directly on the plastic stencil, using a paint brush to spread the pastel over the cutout area. (This method spreads the pastel evenly.) Next, she used gold metallic paint to create the lone star, and red and gold dimensional paints to give some of the fish speckles and stripes.

Designer **Dana Irwin** spotted this crocheted collar in a thrift store and imagined it finding a home on a painted T-shirt for her niece. First she colored the shirt with fabric dyes in funky colors that complement the collar and give the impression of a plaid pattern. Then she sewed on the lavender collar.

L ying around your house are stencils masquerading as something else: a string bag for onions, a fish net, peel-off gold stars, reinforcements for the holes in notebook paper, scraps of paper and masking tape waiting to be torn into jagged shapes. **Saralyn Spradling** rummaged around her house and made a shirt—using all these things, plus fabric paints and a 1-inch (2.5 cm) stenciling brush. She taped or stuck the items on the shirt (starting with masking tape for the shoulder stripes), stenciled paint around them, and ended up with a shirt uniquely hers.

The brassy design on this turquoise shirt also appears on the index page—somewhat clearer, perhaps, in black and violet. **Lenore Davis** drew a full-size design on paper, then glued it to a piece of ³⁄₈-inch (1 cm) foam core. With a craft knife she cut the design out of foam core, glued the pieces to a scrap of mat board about 14 inches (35 cm) square, and trimmed the board around the design. She now had a frottage surface, which she inserted inside the shirt. She used a "dauber," or soft foam ball, to apply the paint (see page 14) to the raised design, using a patting, up and-down motion. For an iridescent effect, she changed from gold to orange to yellow paint.

Lovely painted mountains are surrounded by bursts of light, created by throwing and brushing bleach onto a beige shirt. After the color discharged to her liking, designer **Jean Penland** rinsed the shirt in cold water and then washed it to keep the bleach from destroying the fabric. After the shirt was dry, she drew the shapes of the mountains with fabric pens and painted them in with fabric paints. Next, she framed the landscape with navy fabric paint. Then, with gold and red acrylic paints and a small, flat nylon brush, she added the other design elements.

Peggy DeBell started with a 100 percent black cotton shirt and then, as if by magic, made most of the black disappear. Some black shirts bleach out to an almost white color while others turn a warm brown. First, DeBell ironed the shirt and inserted a cardboard form. She dipped a 1-inch (2.5 cm) foam brush into a solution of 50:50 bleach and tap water, and painted the bleach onto the surface in short strokes, moving the brush in different directions on both the front and back of the shirt. Then she painted the bleach onto the sleeves, using similar strokes. She neutralized the shirt in 50:50 vinegar and tap water, washed, dried, and ironed it. Next, she thinned purple fabric paint and painted it onto the shirt using another foam brush. To outline the purple shapes, she used black fabric marker. She heat-set the paint by ironing it for 5 minutes.

Painting & Embellishing

Ellen Zahorec used transfer fabric crayons to create felines in fanciful hues. First she found a fat cat in a book of iron-on transfer designs and colored it in. (Zahorec decided that, as a grownup, she didn't have to stay inside the lines if she didn't want to.) Next she placed the paper design face-down on a 50:50 cotton-polyester shirt and ironed the back of the paper to transfer the design. She then re-crayoned the sketch and transferred a cat of a different color, continuing until she had an entire litter. With black dimensional paint, Zahorec outlined the cats and added facial features and decorative markings. She also drew a few background accents and filled them with brushed-on fabric paint.

J ust loosen up and paint, says **Amanda Kibler**, who did exactly that when making this shirt. She bought a few bottles of fabric paint at her local craft store and mixed the colors she wanted. Using foam brushes of different sizes (one brush per color, for convenience) and small amounts of paint, she made broad and narrow strokes, swirls, and arches. Then, using plastic pigment extruders, she accented the design in black.

Painting & Embellishing

Because she intended to cover every square inch of fabric, **Betty Kershner** chose to paint this shirt with fiber reactive dyes rather than fabric paints. Since dyes penetrate the fabric, rather than sitting on top, they never add stiffness. Kershner thickened the dyes with sodium alginate, so that they wouldn't run on the fabric. Using a 1-inch (2.5 cm) foam brush, she painted a fantasy landscape, using the end of the brush for lines and overlapping colors when the mood struck her.

Although this black shirt looks as if it's been coated with white paint from a sand-textured roller, the secret to achieving this effect is bleach. **Fleta Monaghan** cut simple stencils out of waxed paper—one of a coffee cup, and another spelling the word "caffiend." She ironed the stencils onto the shirt. Next, she made a diluted solution of bleach and water and put it in a spray bottle. She adjusted the nozzle so that it would spray a very fine mist (test it first on a scrap of fabric). Then she misted the entire shirt, front and back. She neutralized the shirt right away. When she peeled off the waxed paper, the area it blocked remained solid black.

Painting & Embellishing

The blue shirt was treated a little differently from the other shirts designed by **Sandra Holzman** on pages 36 and 37. The white shirt was first vat-dyed blue. Next, Holzman cut a series of stencils in animals shapes and V shapes. When the shirt was dry, she placed the stencils on the front of the shirt and brushed discharge paste inside the cutout areas to remove color. Then she moved each stencil a very small amount and painted them in with blue-gray fabric paint. She used the same stencils on the back of the shirt, but painted in only the shapes.

This happy shirt is simple enough for a child to do, and the results will please everyone. **Liz Hughey** used plastic stencils she purchased in a craft supply store and sponged on blue and yellow stencil fabric paints. With black paint and a fine-tipped brush, she added eyes for the sun and moon. As a finishing touch, she used yellow, blue, and purple fabric markers to accent the stars.

Painting & Embellishing

A woven rush place mat struck **Elma Johnson** as a pattern worth repeating. With masking tape, she taped off a rectangle on the front of a black T shirt, then inserted the place mat inside the shirt, between front and back. She dipped a foam brush in pearlescent textile ink and stroked it gently across the shirt, using the side of the almost-dry brush. As it rubbed against the raised areas of the place mat, the brush painted the woven pattern. Johnson used silver ink to form a frame, orange for the center.

A dark shirt and household bleach can produce a kind of reverse stenciling. **Elma Johnson** drew a pair of giraffes and laid the drawing on six small sheets of freezer paper, stacked shiny side down and stapled together (freezer paper is slippery). She cut around the drawing, producing six paper stencils, which she ironed onto the shirt, again shiny side down. She framed the stencils in masking tape and covered the bottom of the shirt with newspaper. With a mixture of one part household bleach to three parts water in a spray bottle, she sprayed the design. When the shirt faded to a good color, she immediately plunged it into a neutralizing solution—1 cup of vinegar to a gallon of water—to stop the discharge of color.

Painting & Embellishing

Jean Penland combined a number of techniques to create this tree-friendly shirt. First she cut the word "TREES" from a sheet of lacquer film and adhered the stencil to a screen (see page 176 for details). Then she printed the word on the shirt, using acrylic paint mixed to the desired color. Then she wadded a paper towel, dipped it in acrylic paint (several hues of green) and dabbed the paint on the shirt to suggest leaves. Finally, she cut a simplified tree shape from a sponge, brushed fabric paint on it, and printed a row of burgundy trees.

Jean Penland created a star-filled night sky simply by slinging bleach at a navy shirt. When the shirt was bleached to her liking, she rinsed it in cold water and then washed it with a little bit of laundry soap to stop the bleach from eating away at the fabric. When the shirt was dry, she cut a cardboard circle for the moon and painted the outline on the shirt. Then, she brushed on fabric paint to fill in the moon. When the moon was dry, she accented it with dots of gold acrylic paint.

Painting & Embellishing

K. **Lee Manuel's** three daughters are having children these days—and so are her daughter's friends. For each new arrival, Manuel paints a "welcome to the world" shirt. She outlines her designs with a fine-line permanent marker, then paints them with iridescent fabric paints. When the babies move, the designs seem almost as alive as they are.

Earline Hoffmann creates coordinated outfits for all the kids in her family, by painting a plain shirt to match a colorful pair of pants. She mixes fabric paints until the colors match the motif she's chosen. (For this shirt, she mixed red and blue until she got the right pink, yellow and green to match the leaves.) After painting the design, she outlines it with permanent markers.

© 96 Hot Patatoes

Stamping & Block Printing

Stamping or block printing, also called *direct printing*, is probably the oldest and easiest method of producing a repeated image on fabric. The process involves applying color to an object or block and then carefully printing or stamping a design onto the fabric. You can use an object that has a smooth surface and a simple shape, such as half an apple, or a sponge cut into the shape of a heart. Or you can carve or cut a design into the block; the raised areas will print and the recessed areas will not. The irregularities that occur when fabric is block-printed give the piece a distinctive handmade look that is extremely appealing.

Most stamping and printing materials can be found in craft or school supply stores or from mail-order catalogs that carry printing and stamping supplies. You can also make your own stamp pads.

Making the Stamps

■ You can buy rubber stamps in hundreds of patterns from office, art, and craft supply stores as well as from post offices. Choose stamps that have simple details; the more complicated the lines, the less likely you are to have a clear print on fabric.

■ Objects from nature make terrific stamps: a fish (not living, of course!), a cluster of pine needles, a leaf, tree bark, or a piece of a shell all make good stamps. Simply sponge or brush textile paint onto the surface of the object and press it on the shirt.

■ It's easy to make a monotype block that will let you print one single, unique image. Choose an object with a smooth surface—a large rubber eraser, a sanded block of wood, a tile—and apply an even, seamless coat of paint. Then make a design by wiping off some of the paint with the tip of a pencil eraser, a stick, the handle of a spoon, or any other appropriate tool. Plan your design in advance or be spontaneous; either way, work quickly, before the paint dries, then press the carved surface onto the shirt.

■ You can cut simple shapes from cardboard and plastic foam and use them as stamps. Be sure the material is thick enough for you to easily hold onto as you print. It is simple, also, to carve a variety of small, but serviceable stamps from inexpensive white plastic erasers. Use a craft knife to cut out your design.

This giant dragonfly, left, could be a vision from a child's technicolor daydream. The dreamer in this case is **Mary Benagh***, who created the huge rubber stamp, then cut smaller ones to use as accents. She printed the outlines and details of the dragonflies in black. When the paint was dry (about two hours) she colored them in with fabric paints so vibrant that these winged beauties seem ready to fly.*

Stamping & Block Printing

■ Rubber stamping material is a thin sheet of rubber with a peel-off backing. You can use a craft knife to carve a simple or intricate design with raised and recessed areas. When you are satisfied with the design, peel off the backing and adhere the stamp onto something that will give it weight, such as a block of wood.

■ String blocks are a traditional and easy way to print an intriguing design. To make one, glue a piece of cotton string or thin rope across a block of wood in an interesting pattern, creating a three-dimensional raised surface. Press the block into a stamp pad, making sure all sides of the string are covered. When you press the block onto the T-shirt, only the string pattern will print.

■ You can carve a high-quality stamp from a humble potato. Cut one (preferably an Idaho) in half, and let it dry for two hours. Then carve the cut surface. You can carve simple designs and shapes or more intricate ones, such Maya Contento's remarkable birds and berries, on page 87. Maya asserts that her carved potatoes, washed and wrapped in paper towels, last for six days in the refrigerator.

■ Impressive results can be achieved by carving a linoleum block, produced from thin sheets of linoleum glued to a piece of wood. Linoleum is popular for block printing because it yields gently to carving tools and holds up well, even when used frequently. Carving a "lino" block requires some practice, and you will need to purchase a few carving tools. Lino blocks print with even better texture if the carved surface is coated

with flocking, a white, powdery substance. Brush a thin coat of varnish on the raised areas of your carved lino block. Hold a strainer over it and shake a thin layer of flocking onto the wet varnish. Allow to dry; then tap off the excess. Newer carving materials are now available in $\frac{3}{8}$-inch-thick (1 cm) sheets of various sizes. They carve and print much like linoleum, but are softer and much easier to work with.

Applying the Color

You can apply the coloring material to the stamp in a number of ways. To ensure that the printed image is light- and wash-fast on fabric, always use textile products: fabric paints, thickened fiber reactive dyes, or textile inks.

To achieve a painted look, you can brush paint directly onto the stamp, being sure to cover the entire surface evenly. This produces printed images that look painted on, with unique and interesting brush marks. Or you can apply the paint to the stamp with a foam brush, which allows you to put more paint on the stamp, resulting in a strong, clear print. You can also make a stamp pad, using one of the following methods.

METHOD 1

Take a piece of craft felt about 1 foot square (30 cm) and fold it into quarters. Apply a thin layer of fabric paint to the folded felt, making sure the painted area is large enough to cover the area of your stamp.

METHOD 2

To create a padded stamp pad, cover a thin piece of wood or plywood with felt. Brush or brayer the paint onto the felt (a brayer is a rubber roller used for spreading a thin, even layer of paint, as shown in the drawing above).

METHOD 3

Wash and dry a small plastic foam tray (the ones that food comes wrapped in at supermarkets). Place a piece of soft foam rubber about ¼ inch thick (6 mm) in the tray, and use a small spatula to spread fabric paint on both sides of the foam.

Using the Stamp Pad

To use your stamp pad, tap the stamp straight down into the pad several times without twisting it. Test print the image on a paper towel before you tackle the T-shirt. To accelerate drying, you can use a hand-held hair dryer.

Whatever method you use to apply paint to the stamp, here are some tips to successful printing shared by well-known stamp designer Mary Benagh.

■ Insert a cardboard form inside the shirt to protect the side not being printed. Smooth the fabric to eliminate any wrinkles.

■ Start on the back first, so you can practice your technique.

■ If your image is too pale, it means you need more paint on the stamp.

■ If you have too much paint on the stamp, you may get drips on your shirt. Use a brush to soak up any excess paint that builds up on the stamp, particularly around the edges and indentations. If you get paint on the margins of the stamp or on your wooden mount, wipe it clean.

■ Don't let the paint dry on the stamps. Clean them with a mild spray cleaner, warm water, and a fingernail brush.

Stamping & Block Printing

Perfect for the tool man or woman in your life, this navy shirt, designed by **Ellen Zahorec**, is a great beginner stamping project, simple enough for a child to do. Zahorec used precut sponges that she purchased in a craft supply store and printed the shirt with fabric paints in a medley of colors.

How nice to occasionally boil life down to a few of its most basic necessities. That's what these elegant calligraphy stamps do, with their messages of "friend," "flower," and "truth." In keeping with that just the-basics theme, **Lynne Caldwell** used the simplest of techniques to create her striking shirt. She purchased her three rubber stamps at a fabric store, and painted them with charcoal-colored fabric paint before pressing them in place randomly on a rich, red T-shirt.

Stamping & Block Printing

Mary Benagh imitated the look of a woodcut when she cut these rubber stamps of home-sweet-home and birds-on-a-wire. She first printed the images on unbleached cotton fabric. Then she cut out the printed images, folded under the edges of the fabric pieces, and sewed them onto a solid color T-shirt. The secret of the woodcut look is to use plenty of black ink to outline and accent the stamp.

Make an Andy Warhol-like T-shirt for your favorite birthday boy or girl. **Terry Taylor** created his in honor of his brother's 50th. To get the customized stamp, he took one of the birthday boy's old school pictures to a rubber stamp shop and had them create it. (Look under rubber stamps in the phone book; sign shops also often make rubber stamps.) He then used masking tape to mask off four boxes on the shirt, each a little larger than the stamp, and slid a layer of paper between the front and back of the shirt to protect the back from fabric paint. With a small brush, he painted the masked-off boxes with yellow fabric paint. Once the boxes were dry, he loaded the custom stamp with black fabric paint (stamp ink would work, too), and stamped each box. Before adding numbers around the stamped images, he created a paper mask to lay over the central images by stamping onto scrap paper and cutting out the shape. After stamping the numbers, he outlined each central image with dimensional fabric paint. When everything was dry, he masked off one big box to contain the four stamped images, painted it with gold fabric paint, let it dry, then outlined it with 5s and 0s. He finished by heat setting the paints according to the manufacturer's guidelines.

Stamping & Block Printing

Block printing lends itself to simple, stylized designs. **Mary Benagh** ran across some African drawings of animals and decided to adapt them to a T-shirt. From linoleum she carved friendly-looking animals—a fish, a chicken, a turtle, and an aardvark—and a snake whose intentions are questionable.

For most of the animals, Benagh carved two stamps: a solid shape, which she stamped onto the shirt in a bright color; and a more complex surface with cut-out areas in the middle, which she stamped in black, directly over the first color. The cut-out areas of the second stamp allow the colors of the first to show through.

Basic black, she figured, was good enough for the snake.

Astamped image can consist of several individual stamps, such as this ambiable amphibian, designed by **Mary Benagh**. She cut the components from rubber-stamping material and printed each piece with fabric paints in primary colors. The result is an eye-popping gathering of tree frogs (plus a few flies for lunch!).

Stamping & Block Printing

A diamond cut from a sheet of rubber-stamp material was the starting point for this lively child's shirt, designed by **Jean Penland**. First she cut four diamonds of the same size from the rubber. She glued them in a stack to make a thick stamp, and glued the layered rubber diamond to a block of wood. She printed diamonds on the shirt with multi-layers of fabric paint. Then, with a ½-inch (1.5 cm) brush and fabric paint, she added the rectangles. She let the shirt dry for 30 minutes and then washed it in the sink: the centers of the shapes that were not yet dry washed out, leaving an interesting random pattern. Next, Penland cut a sponge in the shape of a fish, brushed on fabric paint, and printed it on the shirt. As a final accent, she dipped the butt of the brush in paint and speckled the shirt.

M aya Contento creates
marvelously intricate
designs on T-shirts by stamping
with carved potatoes. She recom-
mends Idaho potatoes because
they stay firmer longer and print
exceedingly well. First she cuts the
potatoes in half lengthwise with a
sharp knife. She "draws" her design
into the potato using a craft knife with a triangular blade. Then she cuts out this design to make a thicker
line so that the details will be clear when printed. Finally, she cuts off any part of the potato that is outside
of the stamp she is creating.

Using fabric paints, she brushes all the details onto the potato stamp. She presses the potato firmly
onto the shirt and removes it quickly. For each image, she repaints the potato. This Wild Goose design,
one of Contento's favorites, features two of her pets, a cat and a dachshund, curled up on one sleeve.

Stamping & Block Printing

Occasionally, somebody else is good enough to create a stamp for you—like the post office, for example. **Cyndi Fox** decided the messages on these rubber stamps were at least as relevant to people as to merchandise, so she put them on a shirt. A similar one is easy to make.

For the stripes, use fabric paint and a small foam paint roller, available at most hardware stores. (Fox's was 2½ inches, or 6 cm, wide.) Pour a little paint into a disposable pie pan and roll the roller back and forth until it's covered. Starting in the center of the shirt, lightly roll the paint from neck to hem, then go back and fill in the stripe as necessary. Rinse out the pan and roller (dry the pan and squeeze the roller with paper towels) each time you change colors. Allow the finished stripes to dry.

Brush a thin film of black fabric paint on a folded square of craft felt, to create a stamp pad. Lightly touch the stamp to the felt, and print the words across the shoulders.

Fish turn up regularly on textiles, tombstones, and **Peggy DeBell's** T shirts. To print her porgy, she gutted it (but left the scales) and laid it on a piece of foam core, so she could pin the fins and tail open. She brushed a light coat of fabric paint onto the fish, placed a T-shirt on top, and rubbed gently.

To create the stripes of color, DeBell used a 5-inch (12 cm) paint roller. She brushed stripes of paint around the roller, and rolled it onto the shirt. She carved a rectangular lino block and stamped it in black. To accent, she used markers and a small sponge brush.

Stamping & Block Printing

Sometimes the simplest shapes are the most satisfying. **Mary Benagh** carved four different pitchers out of linoleum, brushed fabric paint onto them, and stamped a T-shirt that's ready for entertaining. The brush marks on the blocks left their imprint on the shirt, adding interesting texture.

The message of this shirt is, never stop too soon. **Ellen Zahorec** carved and flocked a large linoleum block and stamped it across the shirt in navy blue textile ink. The block is easiest to spot at the bottom of the shirt: it's printed three times, side by side. It extends from the navy triangles at the very bottom to halfway up around the lime green hexagons. Midway up the green hexagons the block appears again in a row of three—this time, upside down. (Look for the navy blue.)

Zahorec outlined the block prints in yellow and red dimensional paint, and filled in the empty spaces within the design with fabric paint: neon yellow, pink, orange, green, and turquoise. Squeeze-bottle paint with metallic threads added texture, and fabric pens added polka dots—pink, purple, and pale blue.

Stamping & Block Printing

Gum erasers and jar lids make terrific stamps, as **Ellen Zahorec** discovered. She pressed the jar lid into black fabric paint to print circles on the shirt. Then she filled in the circles with fabric paint, some in glitter colors, overlapping them to create her design. Next she dabbed the ends of the erasers in black paint and stamped the shirt, leaving interesting textural marks that resemble fingerprints.

Made to resemble a woodcut, this star–gazer's fantasy was created by **Mary Benagh**, who cut the entire image from one very large sheet of rubber-stamp material. Then she cut two stamps depicting shooting stars and printed them as a motif to accent the central image. Starlight, star bright, may I have this wish tonight!

Stamping & Block Printing

If you're going to carve a lino block, you might as well get more than one shirt out of it. So says **Ellen Zahorec**, who re-used the block from the previous page. This time she chose a coral shirt and printed the block in purple. She also carved a second, simpler block and used it to print over the first. She printed the bottom of the shirt in burnt orange, then added white to her paint as she moved toward the top. With a brush and some fabric paint—blue, pink, orange, purple, and metallic turquoise—she filled in some of the empty spaces.

Remember the profound, squishy pleasure of finger painting? Monotype blocks bring it all back. **Lenore Davis** pressed a smooth wooden block about 3 inches (7.5 cm) square into a stamp pad, covering it with an even coat of paint, then used a mini spatula and a small, sharp-edged eraser to wipe a design into the paint. She printed the block, then wiped it off and started again. With the edges she printed a narrow border, then painted a darker blue diamond in the center.

Stamping & Block Printing

Ellen Zahorec created this attractive shirt by printing with kitchen tools and other household items, such as spatulas, forks, a tape dispenser—even a credit card. She spread textile paints on paper plates. Then she tapped each object in the paint and printed the image on the shirt. She used the edge of the credit card to add white lines to emphasize the pleasing geometric look of the design.

Leaves make wonderful stamps to use on fabric. Designer **Ellen Zahorec** rolled out textile paints on paper plates. She gently pressed a leaf in the paint and placed it on the shirt. Next, she covered the leaf with a paper napkin and smoothed it with her fingers. She removed the paper and the leaf and continued printing the shirt with different leaves, using different colors. She overlapped the leaves to create a woodland effect.

Stamping & Block Printing

Using white opaque fabric paint and a stamp carved from an eraser, **Cyndi Fox** created intricate diagonal stripes across a black shirt. Each diagonal band consists of two rows of side-by-side images. Since the stamp was small— 2 inches by 1½ inches (5 x 1¾ cm), a lot of stamping went into this dressy shirt.

Found objects and fabric paint helped **Peggy DeBell** produce this striking shirt. To make a similar one, gather a few flat items and begin. Lay a paper doily at strategic points on the shirt, apply black paint to a 5-inch (12.5 cm) paint roller, and roll it over the doily, to leave a lacy impression. (Use a napped roller, to print less paint.) Brush fabric paint on a ginkgo leaf and press the painted side gently into the shirt. Repeat with other leaves and other colors. When the paint is dry, use a fabric marker to outline the leaves and sketch in the veins. Finally, apply a thin coat of paint to the roller and roll it lightly across the shirt, to produce the sponged-looking background.

Stamping & Block Printing

This charming long-sleeved T features enough cups of java to satisfy even the most ardent coffee lover. **Mary Benagh's** stamps of coffee cups and saucers are bordered by a simple geometric pattern printed in black, and accented with a small floral stamp, printed in blue.

A warm, tempting break-fast (stamped, of course), was cooked up by **Mary Benagh**, who designs and markets a line of rubber stamps and kits through her company, Hot Potatoes.®

Stamping & Block Printing

Mary **Benagh** combined five of her rubber stamps on this shirt to create a design that might tempt a friendly bird to nest. These charming birdhouse stamps, which Benagh sells as part of her product line, can be reproduced from rubber-stamp material. Use simple lines and details when you cut the stamps, and print them in your favorite colors.

Maya **Contento** loves to combine a cornucopia of fruits and vegetables on fantasy vines. A pair of flickers, lizards, and a smiling moon look on approvingly. All the images were carved from potatoes, as described on page 71.

Stamping & Block Printing

Wanna be the only aunt or uncle your nieces and nephews really like? Give them the moon—along with Saturn, the Milky Way, and a host of stars, not to mention rockets and spaceships to get there in. **Mary Benagh** carved a few linoleum blocks, brushed them with vibrant fabric paint, and stamped an exuberant Space Age shirt.

Stamping & Block Printing

For that fantasy safari, carve a jungleful of wild animals from a pound of potatoes. Designer **Mary Benagh** claims that, once you've stamped a parade of brilliant beasts, you'll have created the favorite shirt of a favorite child.

Stamping & Block Printing

Like the hot coffee it celebrates, this shirt will get you going in the morning. To begin, **Peggy DeBell** cut two lino blocks—one for the coffee cup and one for the rectangular shape. She painted them with iridescent acrylic fabric paint, and printed them on the shirt. Using purchased letter stencils and a stenciling brush, she added words and exclamation points. Finally, she cut a heart shape from a piece of cardboard and stenciled lavender hearts up and down the center.

For a baroque shirt, **Ellen Zahorec** carved a large, elaborate lino block about 6 inches wide and 9 inches high (15 x 22.5 cm) and printed it six times: three times across the top and another three directly underneath. (The bottom row is upside down.) To complete the design, she printed the end of the block at the right and left borders.

Since the black textile ink produced an interesting but subdued design, Zahorec resorted to color. She outlined parts of the design in purple and rust dimensional paint, then went back with a brush and fabric paints in hot pink, turquoise, and metallic mauve.

Tie-Dye

Certainly one of the most popular methods of giving life to a plain T-shirt, tie-dyeing also remains one of the easiest forms of what is called bound resist dyeing. No matter how you approach tie-dyeing, it's almost impossible to mess up; if the design turns out differently than you planned, who will know? You'll still end up with something you can wear, and you'll probably even get compliments on it!

The secret to creating any sort of pattern—intentional or not—lies primarily in the "tie"-ing part of the game. Very simply, how you tie your T-shirt affects how your design will turn out. It works like this: you take a clean shirt and ball, fold, pleat, scrunch, or twist it. Then you bind up your wad of cloth and you're ready to go! Whatever fabric remains on the inside of your knotted mass, where dye can't reach it, will retain its original color. This creates contrast with the material on the outside of the fabric, which will be exposed to the dye. Thus, the pattern you end up with will vary depending on how you tie, or bind, your shirt.

Tying and Binding

There are many ways and means of binding a shirt to create designs. Successful binding materials include string, rubber bands, twist ties, waxed nylon cord, and C-clamps.

Random tying and binding

Stitching and folding the shirt sleeve

To create the colorful blossoms in Monet's Garden Revisited, *left, designer* **Tye Dye Mary® (Mary Patricia Deprez)** *used the spider-walk technique, crimping and scrunching a flat T-shirt into a ½-inch (1.5 cm) tall bundle. She wrapped the bundle fairly loosely with a long piece of string tied in a cross-hatch pattern, creating a semi-limp, skillet-sized pancake. Using an eyedropper, she applied dye in diagonal stripes on either side of the shirt until very little white was visible. Finally, she machine-rinsed the shirt to strip the dye, heat-set the fabric with a mild dish-washing detergent, and let it tumble dry. While still damp, she laid the shirt flat to shape and dry.*

93

You can tie the cloth, wrap it around wood and bind it with clamps, or stitch the cloth in segments with a needle and thread, as shown in the drawing on page 93.

Dyes

Almost all tie-dyers use fiber reactive dyes. Not only are these easy to use dyes light- and wash-fast, they also yield brilliant colors at room temperature, meaning there's no hassle with boiling dye baths. The catch to using these dyes is that they work well only on natural fibers, so make sure the tag on your T-shirt says 100 percent cotton.

Most commonly sold as powders, fiber reactive dyes are also available in liquid form. Either form remains inert until dissolved in an alkaline solution. Therefore, to use fiber reactive dyes, you will also need a separate packet of powdered "fixer" or "activator," technically known as sodium carbonate, and commonly called washing soda, soda ash, or sal soda (it looks exactly like laundry detergent). The fixer can be added to the dye at various times, depending on the technique you're using.

While adding color to a shirt by dyeing it is the most obvious way to create designs, taking color away achieves remarkable results, too. Discharge dyeing, removing color from fabric, ranks as a popular technique among tie-dyers. Start with a dark fabric (such as black or purple), bind the shirt as you like, and then apply bleach to it, either by immersion, or by brushing or spraying it on the shirt.

Applying the Dyes

Getting the dye onto the T-shirt can be as fun and creative as you make it. You can dunk your tied shirt in a bucket of dye for a fast and thorough approach, or you can apply dyes directly to the shirt with a host of objects, including paintbrushes, eyedroppers, turkey basters, spray bottles, spoons, and plastic syringes. Your method of choice will vary depending on how much dye you want on your shirt and where you want it (some dyeing tools offer more control than others).

There are innumerable dye recipes and procedures for tie-dyeing fabric, and professional designers usually have their own tailor-made methods and formulas that work for them. Here are just a few procedures we've found to be successful. (As always, check the dye package for directions first.) For most methods, you'll need two clean buckets.

PRESOAKING

Using this method, you can soak the shirt in soda ash first and add the dye later, which means you can use different colors of dye in the same application.

1. Dissolve 1 cup (236.6 ml) of soda ash in a gallon (3.785 l) of water, and soak the shirt until it's saturated.

2. Remove the shirt and tie it as desired.

3. Dissolve 1 teaspoon (4.9 ml) of dye in $\frac{1}{2}$ cup (118.3 ml) of water. To avoid lumps, add 1 tablespoon (14.8 ml) of the water to the dye powder and stir until you have a smooth paste. Then gradually stir in the rest of the water.

4. Apply the dye directly onto the shirt.

5. Put the shirt in a plastic bag (to keep it damp), and let it sit for 24 hours.

6. Rinse the shirt carefully, especially if you've used more than one color. Hold one end of it under running water, then the middle, then the other end. Undo the ties and rinse again.

7. Soak the shirt in a pan of very hot, soapy water for 10 minutes. Rinse until the water runs clear, and lay the shirt flat to dry.

DIRECT APPLICATION

Sometimes it's more convenient to have the fixer in the dye solution itself.

1. Dissolve 1 teaspoon (4.9 ml) of dye in ½ cup (118.3 ml) of water.

2. Stir 4 teaspoons (19.6 ml) of soda ash into the dye solution.

3. Apply the dye mixture directly onto the shirt.

4. Store in a plastic bag (to keep it damp) for 24 hours.

5. Rinse carefully.

IMMERSION

In this method, the amount of dye powder you'll need depends on the weight of the fabric you're dyeing. For every 100 grams (3.5 oz) of fabric (just about the weight of an adult T-shirt), you'll need the following:

- 3 quarts water (2.838 l) + ½ cup (118.3 ml)

- ¼ cup (59.1 ml) salt

- 1 teaspoon (4.9 ml) dye

- 4 teaspoons (19.6 ml) soda ash

1. Fold and bind a clean, wet shirt.

2. Dissolve the dye in ½ cup (118.3 ml) of water.

3. Make the dye bath. Put a gallon (3.785 l) of water in a bucket, add the salt, and stir until dissolved. Add the dissolved dye.

4. Immerse the bound shirt in the bath and stir it gently for 15 minutes.

5. Remove the shirt and stir in the soda ash.

6. Return the shirt to the dye bath for 30 minutes, stirring occasionally.

7. Rinse the shirt using lukewarm water (do not use ice-cold water), remove the bindings, and rinse again. For the final rinse, use a soap-based detergent to rinse out the excess dye.

8. Lay flat to dry.

Tie-Dye

Safety Tips

Although making tie-dyes may feel like fun and games, remember that you are working with industrial chemicals and take basic precautions to avoid accidents.

■ Wear a dust mask to avoid inhaling dyes in powdered form. The dye particles are easily airborne, meaning they're easy to inhale or send through your home's heating system. Don't leave opened tins of dye lying around. Uncover dyes only when you are ready to make them liquid, then re-cover them immediately.

■ Wear rubber gloves when handling dyes, wet or dry. Your skin will absorb the colors wonderfully, making you look as tie-dyed as your T-shirt.

■ Your skin is not a T-shirt, however. If you do dye it, don't attempt to bleach it out with household bleach. Scrub your skin with soap and a nail brush and wait for the dye to fade (usually not longer than a day or two).

■ Don't use the same utensils for dyeing and for cooking. While spoons may make an appropriate tool for tie-dyeing, dye may not be the secret ingredient you want in your soup.

Patterns

Many tie-dye patterns exist in the T-shirt world. Some of the most popular have come to be known by name. To give you some idea of how these specific patterns are created, we've included step-by-step instructions for creating the patterns known as the diamond, the double spiral, the rainbow yoke, and the lightning bolt.

1. Fold the shirt vertically, then horizontally.

2. Accordion fold the shirt from center to shoulders.

3. Dye in alternating rows of black and gray.

DIAMOND

1. Wash the T-shirt and lay it, still damp, on a flat work surface. Fold it in half vertically, matching the sides and shoulder. Then, about 1½ inches (4 cm) below the armpit, fold it in half horizontally.

2. Accordion-fold the entire shirt from the center (it's at the lower left corner of the folded shirt) to the shoulders. Bind tightly, using pieces of string every inch (2.5 cm) or so.

3. Using eyedroppers or a plastic bottle, apply the dye in rows of drops perpendicular to the folds, alternating rows of two colors. Turn the shirt over and repeat the process, but reverse the order of the colors.

4. Carefully put the shirt in a plastic bag, and let it sit for 24 hours. Rinse, wash, and dry.

DOUBLE SPIRAL

1. Presoak the shirt in a solution of soda ash and water.

2. Lay the shirt on a flat surface, and smooth out all wrinkles.

3. Fold the shirt in half diagonally—the shirt's right hip over its left shoulder.

4. With pliers, pinch the shirt at the point where you want the center of the spiral. (Actually, this will be the center of both spirals.) The pliers will help you keep hold of the shirt as it twists.

5. During this next step, the shirt continues to lie on the table. With the other hand, start to twist the shirt. Stop periodically to keep the folds neat and even. Twist until the shirt forms a flat disc.

6. Slide three to six rubber bands around the disc. If it curls up, use fewer or looser rubber bands.

7. Make the dye solutions (1 teaspoon of dye in ½ cup of water) and put each color in a squeeze bottle.

8. Place the shirt on a stack of paper towels or newspapers, and apply dye directly to the shirt. Dye the top side in pie-shaped wedges from the center to the edge: yellow, light blue, azure blue, purple, red, and orange. Carefully turn the disc over and dye the other side black.

1. Fold the shirt diagonally.

2. Hold the shirt with one hand, and twist it with the other.

3. Dye one side in pie-shaped wedges.

9. Place the dyed shirt in a plastic bag, with the rainbow side up, and leave it for 24 hours.

10. Remove the shirt from the bag and remove the rubber bands. Rinse, untie the shirt, rinse again, and soak in hot water and laundry detergent. Rinse, and lay flat to dry.

RAINBOW YOKE

1. Wash the shirt and lay it flat, still damp. Smooth out the wrinkles and fold it vertically, matching up sides and sleeves. Working from shoulder to belly, accordion fold the shirt diagonally into 1-inch (2.5 cm) pleats. Tie the shirt tightly, covering the area where you want the rainbow yoke to fall.

2. Prepare the dye solutions for direct application, mixing soda ash into the dye itself. Using eye droppers, apply dye in stripes across the folds: purple, then red, orange, yellow, green, and blue. Turn the shirt over and repeat the dyeing, shifting the color spectrum over one band: red, orange, yellow, green, blue, purple, and red. After the stripes are done, dye the rest of the shirt turquoise, using a plastic baster.

3. Lay the shirt flat on a plastic-lined baking sheet, cover with plastic, and allow it to sit for 24 hours.

1. Fold the shirt vertically.

2. Accordion fold it from shoulder to belly.

3. Tie it and dye it in rainbow stripes.

LIGHTNING BOLT

1. With a pencil or washable marker, draw a zigzag line on the shirt. This line will be the center of the lightning bolt.

2. Thread a needle with a long piece of nylon thread, and tie a large knot at the end. Baste along the penciled lightning bolt, using ¼-inch (6 mm) stitches.

3. Keeping the shirt flat on the table, pull the thread, thus gathering the center of the shirt into the desired design. Tie a large knot, and clip the thread ends.

4. Soak the shirt in water and soda ash, and wring it out.

5. Place the shirt on a flat surface. Pull the ends of the fabric until the folds are uniform in height.

6. Tie two pieces of cotton string around the shirt, about ½ inch (1 cm) on either side of the nylon thread. Put rubber bands around the rest of the shirt.

7. Apply dye from squeeze bottles. Use white dye between the pieces of string (check directions on dye packet for "clear"), red on one end of the fabric, blue on the other.

8. Put the shirt in a plastic bag and leave it for 24 hours.

9. Cut strings and rubber bands, and remove nylon thread. Rinse the shirt in cold water and laundry detergent until the water is clear.

1. Baste along the penciled lightning bolt.

2. Gather the center.

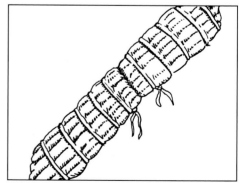

3. Bind the shirt and dye it.

The brilliant colors in this tie-dyed shirt are compliments of **Michael Smith**, who started with a black one. Using the fingers of both hands, he "scrunched" the clean, wet shirt into tight folds, wrinkling and folding until it was about a foot across and about an inch high (30 x 2.5 cm). After binding it with rubber bands to hold the shape, he immersed it in a bleach solution until the exposed folds were very pale, then plunged it in a neutralizing solution. He vat-dyed the shirt brilliant blue, then rinsed and laundered it. Starting with a clean black-and-blue shirt, he re-scrunched, re-bleached, and re-dyed, this time using a vivid red.

A professional designer, Smith has to worry about large production runs, which means vat dyeing. If you're dyeing only a shirt or two, there's an easier alternative. After you've scrunched and bound the shirt, use a spray bottle to spray the bleach solution onto the exposed folds, on both the front and back sides of the shirt. When the folds are light enough, immerse the shirt in a neutralizing solution. Then apply the first color dye to the folds with a plastic bottle or an eye dropper. After carefully rinsing and laundering the shirt, repeat the entire process for the second color.

Tie-Dye

Lynne Caldwell has come up with an easy way to dip into the ancient Japanese art of shibori—a method of stitching (or otherwise binding) and dyeing that's the precursor of modern tie-dye. Instead of decorating an entire T-shirt, she dyed small swatches of silk, then used them as embellishments. For the top swatch, she used a doubled strand of quilter's thread to create a simple running stitch, then bound the silk tightly by pulling up both ends of thread and knotting them once the swatch squished together like an accordion. She soaked the silk for 30 minutes in marigold acid dye (which is better for silk than fiber-reactive dye). She repeated the technique for the middle panel, but used leaf-green dye. For the swatch on the bottom, she created round bursts by wrapping popcorn kernels in the silk swatch before soaking it in marigold dye. To combine the three pieces into one panel, she sewed them to the center of the shirt, then sewed on a border of antique ribbon, and finished the design with accents of tiny gold seed beads to mimic the popcorn pattern.

Betty Kershner created a beautiful and unique look by combining tie-dye and appliqué. First she folded a white T-shirt in triangles accordion-style, using C-clamps to secure it between pieces of wood. After wetting the fabric around the wood and squeezing out excess water, she immersed the shirt in light blue dye. She then rinsed and washed the shirt until the water ran clear, re-bound it, and performed a second immersion, this time using pink dye. After a second rinsing, she let the shirt dry for 24 hours and then washed it in hot water. As a final touch, Kershner sewed on a batiked motif (a motif from any purchased fabric will do) using a zigzag stitch, trimming the edges of the material close to the zigzag line.

Tie-Dye

Rainbow colors make this traditional pattern especially eye-catching.
Tye Dye Mary® (**Mary Patricia Deprez**) accordion-pleated the
shirt from shoulder to belly, used eye droppers to
dye the large V, then dyed the rest of the
shirt turquoise. For tying instructions,
see page 99.

The double spiral is one of the most enduring tie-dye patterns. **Timothy Putney** dyed this one in brilliant colors with contrasting black accents. For binding instructions, see page 98.

Tie-Dye

To achieve this stunning combination of black and blue, **Mystic Eye** designers crinkled a wet, white T-shirt into tight, even mountains about $\frac{1}{2}$ an inch (1.5 cm) high. Then they dyed the shirt twice, first black, then blue, and laundered it to set the colors.

Ever wondered what the surface of the sun looks like? We think this fiery tie-dye by Chaos designers **Michael Smith** and **Cole Cannizaro** comes close to the real thing. The designers started with a wet, purple T-shirt and worked backwards. First they bound the shirt. Next they performed a series of discharge techniques to remove its original color. Last, they applied successive layers of dye to give it its on-fire effect.

Michael Smith folded and pleated a black shirt until he had a convoluted mass about a foot across and an inch high (30 x 2.5 cm). After binding it with rubber bands, he immersed it in a bleach solution until the exposed folds were as light as he could get them, then neutralized and laundered the shirt. He re-tied and re-bleached the shirt twice more, dyeing the bleached folds light blue the first time and azure blue the second.

JoAnn Giordano used the Japanese technique of shibori to create a soft, blurry-edged pattern. First she wrapped a black shirt around a length of 6-inch-diameter (15 cm) PVC pipe, starting with the top of the shirt at the top of the pipe. She then bound it tightly with string, spiraling down the shirt so the bindings were about an inch (2.5 cm) apart.

Next, Giordano compressed the fabric on the pipe, pushing the bottom end of the shirt toward the top, twisting as she pushed. She then wet the shirt and immersed it, pole and all, in a bleach solution and left it there until she liked the degree of discharge. She removed the shirt from the pole, rinsed it well, and neutralized it for 10 minutes in a sodium bisulfite solution.

Tie-Dye

Mystic Eye designers tie-dyed this white T-shirt in yellow, blue, and red dyes to bring forth every color of the rainbow. They crinkled the wet shirt into tight, even mountains about ½ inch (1.5 cm) high. Then they bound the shirt onto a form and applied the three dyes in succession. As a final step, they laundered the shirt to set its brilliant hues for good.

Remember the crayon drawings you did as a kid, where you covered the entire picture with a layer of black crayon, and scraped it off in designs to reveal the bright colors underneath? **Michael Smith** and **Cole Cannizaro** achieved a similar effect in this gorgeous tie-dye. The Chaos designers started with a wet, black T-shirt, then bound the fabric and lightened it through a series of discharge techniques. Last, they applied successive layers of color to the shirt, which show up magnificently in the absence of black.

Tie-Dye

Even in a subdued color scheme of black, gray, and white, this diamond shaped pattern is arresting. **Tye Dye Mary® (Mary Patricia Deprez)** folded a white shirt in quarters, accordion pleated and tied it, then dyed alternating stripes of black and gray. For complete instructions, see page 97.

Timothy Putney started with a white shirt, but aimed to electrify. A lightning bolt in red, white, and blue sizzles across his shirt. For binding instructions, see page 100.

Who says the world's not flat? The globe takes on two dimensions in the brilliant blues and greens of this shirt by **Tye Dye Mary® (Mary Patricia Deprez)**. She created the v-shape pattern of *Blues on Green Yoke* by smoothing the T-shirt and folding it in half. Next, she folded it accordion style on a diagonal and bound it with string. Using a direct application technique, she applied dye to the bound shirt in stripes. To set the design, first she machine-rinsed the shirt, then she heat-set the fabric with a mild dish-washing soap, and last, she let the shirt tumble dry. As a final step, Deprez laid the shirt flat to shape and dry completely.

Striking beams of light shimmer on a purple backdrop in **Betty Kershner's** handsome creation. After initially folding, clamping, and bleaching the shirt, she laid it out flat on a plastic surface. Using a foam paintbrush, she applied light yellow dye to highlight the bleached design on the front and back of the shirt. To cure the dye, Kershner washed the shirt in hot water after it had been dry for 24 hours.

Reminiscent of a cave painting, this shirt combines tie-dye and screen printing. **Susan Baylies** used a lacquer film stencil to print the women and animals, using black paint on the left of the screen and rust brown on the right. But first she tie-dyed the background. She wadded and wrapped a wet shirt into a ball, tucking the tail end into the center so it held its shape. She put the shirt into a bucket, weighted it down with a dinner plate so it wouldn't float, and covered it with blue dye (water, powder, and fixer). After the shirt had soaked for about 30 minutes, she removed it from the bath, unwadded and re-wadded it, and immersed it in green dye. The final re-wadding was for purple. Finally, she rinsed the shirt carefully.

Tye Dye Mary® (**Mary Patricia Deprez**) calls this shirt *Amethyst Crystal*. To make it, she laid a white shirt flat on her work surface and smoothed out the wrinkles. Then she "spiderwalked" her fingers across the shirt, pinching and scrunching until it consisted of $\frac{1}{2}$-inch-high (1 cm) convolutions. She wrapped the bundle fairly loosely with a long piece of string, creating a kind of semi limp, skillet-sized pancake. With an eye dropper, she cross-hatched lines of purple dye across the top until very little white was visible, then turned the shirt over and repeated the process. After letting the shirt sit in a plastic bag for 24 hours, she rinsed, washed, and dried it.

Tie-Dye

While the design on this tie-dye may appear to be the work of random hands singing the praises of chaos, designers **Michael Smith** and **Cole Cannizaro** actually use special, custom-designed equipment to achieve their unique results. However, you can get something similar by hand. The designers bound and dyed a wet, black T-shirt in a discharge solution. They then applied several layers of color to the fabric to highlight its unusual patterns.

To create this majestic shirt— an exciting example of discharge dyeing— the designers at **The Mystic Eye** started with a wet, pink shirt. Then, using the fingers of both hands, they crinkled the fabric into tight, even "mountains" about ½ inch (1.5 cm) high. The shirt was bound onto a form and immersed in bleach. The bleach was then neutralized and the shirt laundered. The entire process was repeated twice more using light orange and violet dyes to achieve this wonderful blend of colors.

Tie-Dye

Electric green and blue dyes spider-walk their way across this shirt. **Michael Smith** accordion-folded a black shirt into an inch-high (2.5 cm) mass, secured it with rubber bands, and bleached the exposed folds into pale, curving lines. After neutralizing the shirt, he immersed it in blue dye, which colored the bleached areas. After rinsing, unbinding, and laundering the shirt, he repeated the folding-bleaching-dyeing process, this time using a bright green dye.

The blue lines of color on this shirt shimmer like sunlight on the sandy bottom of the sea. **Michael Smith** followed the procedure described on page 120, but this time he used a color scheme of blue and brown.

Batik

Batik is another method of applying colored designs to fabric by covering certain sections with a substance, usually liquid wax, so that they retain the original color of the fabric when it is dyed. The wax, (or sometimes rice paste or mud) is the resist. Melted wax is poured or brushed onto the fabric where it penetrates deep into the weave. When the wax cools, it hardens in place and repels the dye.

Depending on the number of wax applications and dye immersions, the fabric can be monochrome or multicolored. If the fabric is waxed before it is dyed, its original color will be part of the design. Areas that have been dyed already can be waxed and overdyed. If, for example, you wish to illustrate a bank of clouds in a blue sky, you would wax cloud shapes on a white T-shirt and immerse it in a blue dye bath. When you remove the wax, you will have white clouds on a blue sky. If you want to add a blue boat on a turquoise ocean, you would wax a boat shape on the bottom portion of the shirt and immerse the bottom of the shirt in a green dye bath. When you remove the wax, you will have a blue boat on a sea the color of blue overdyed with green. Mixing colors in this way is one of the appealing aspects of batik, but it's important that you understand how each dye color will affect the color it overdyes, and plan the sequence of dyes before you apply the wax to the shirt.

Unless you are extremely careful, the smooth wax will crack when the fabric is immersed in the cold dye bath. The dye penetrates those hairline cracks, leaving spider web lines of color. Many batikers deliberately aim for this effect or look kindly on their mistakes, and this "crackle" has become a trademark of batik.

Wax

The quality of the resist depends mostly on the types and combinations of the waxes. Beeswax, the traditional batik resist, is strong and durable, but is not resistant to alkali, and can cause surprising breaks when dyed. Its synthetic equivalent, microcrystalline wax, adheres and penetrates the fabric easily. Paraffin wax has a lower melting point, is thin, and tends to crack or flake off the fabric, which means the batik will be heavily veined. Some batikers use resins and fats in combination with waxes. Most craft stores

*As an adult, **George Summers, Jr.** has always lived near an ocean. Since childhood, he's been intrigued by mermaids. How were these sirens of the sea able to warn sailors of a rocky shoreline or send them to their doom? He also was intrigued by the idea of dyeing a batik in varying shades of the same color. The overdyeing in this shirt, left, was turquoise, bright blue, and royal blue (see details on page 125).*

sell granulated batik wax, a combination of paraffin and microcrystalline waxes in the ratio 2:1, which creates a desirable medium crackle. You can experiment by adding a little more or less of an individual wax to see what the results are like.

*This is the back of the mermaid shirt designed by **George Summers, Jr.** Note how her tail wraps around the shirt.*

Wax Melter

You have to heat the wax so that it liquifies and penetrates the fabric. If the wax merely sits on the surface, the dye will run under it and blur the lines of your design.

To melt the wax you need a heavy metal pan or pot, thermostatically controlled, with a stable base. An electric skillet or a small deep-fat fryer work well. Don't use appliances with only on-off switches because the temperature, which needs to remain constant, can't be controlled. A fall-back option is a double boiler with a water compartment, but the wax, although it will melt, may not get hot enough to adequately penetrate the fabric.

The key here is to heat the wax slowly and gradually, without overheating it, and to maintain a constant temperature once the wax has melted. Never heat wax over an open flame as it may catch fire. Never leave melting wax unattended. Keep children and pets away from melting wax. If the wax starts to smoke or the brush sizzles when you dip it in the wax, immediately reduce the heat.

Brushes

You will need a number of brushes for applying wax and dye. Use inexpensive ones for waxing because you won't be able to use them for any other purpose once they're covered in wax. Choose brushes with stiff bristles, which helps to push the wax into the weave.

For applying dye, choose narrow and broad brushes so you will have the right tool both for painting in individual sections of a design and for coloring in the background. Brushing on dye allows you to use more color selection than if you immerse the fabric in a dye bath. The best brushes are made of hair and are tightly packed and absorbent. For small areas, a watercolor brush works well. Dyes penetrate easily, so you will need to clean the brushes thoroughly in a mild detergent and dry them.

Tjanting

A *tjanting* is a small, spouted metal cup on the end of a heat-proof wooden handle, used to apply the molten wax. It comes in many sizes. The melted wax can be poured from the tjanting onto the fabric to form fine, precise lines or small dots, or to fill in solid sections. This inexpensive, traditional tool is sold in most good craft or art-supply stores. With a little practice, you will soon be adept at controlling the outflow of the wax using this time-tested tool.

Dye

For batik, you must use fiber reactive, cold-water dyes: a hot dye bath would melt the wax and ruin the design. Dye can be applied either by immersing the shirt in the dye bath or by painting on the dye with a brush.

Step By Step

1. Use only a 100 percent cotton shirt. Wash it in a mild dish-washing soap to remove the sizing.

2. Stretch the T-shirt on a batik frame or an artist's canvas stretcher. Or insert a sheet of cardboard inside the shirt to make it taut. Another approach is to simply lay the shirt

George Summers, Jr. used a pencil to lightly sketch the design of St. Francis on the cotton. Then he waxed around certain areas, such as the clouds, the face, and the hand. Here he uses a brush to paint dye inside these areas enclosed by wax.

flat and slip newspapers covered with a piece of waxed paper inside.

3. Prepare the dye—either a stock solution for painting or a dye bath.

4. Heat the wax until it flows like water. Test it on a scrap of cotton fabric. If it looks transparent, it's ready to use. If it's still opaque, heat it more. Waxes melt at different temperatures—mostly around 100° to 150°F (38° to 65°C), and their flash points range from 400° to 500°F (204° to 260°C). One approach is to set the thermostat on your wax-melting pot or pan to 150°F (65°C) and increase it by 10°F until the wax penetrates the fabric—usually about 270°F (132°C). Steer clear of the flash point!

The fabric, with the face and hand dyed, is immersed in yellow dye to color in the sky.

5. Using a tjanting or brush, apply wax to those areas you want to remain undyed and let the wax dry.

6. Apply the dye. If you are immersing the shirt, keep it as flat as possible so the wax doesn't crack unintentionally. If you want the hairline cracks, gently crumple the waxed areas before immersing the shirt. Painting on the dye works best for small areas enclosed by wax; these islands of fabric will hold the dye and prevent it from bleeding into other areas. To paint open areas, thicken the dye with sodium alginate (see page 12). You can paint on undyed sections of the T-shirt or over other dyes to modify the color.

7. Place the shirt flat to dry on newspapers covered with wax paper or plastic. Don't hang the shirt because the dye may run to the bottom and make the color uneven.

Summers uses a tjanting to outline the leaves with wax.

8. When the shirt is dry, wax other areas for a second color, if you desire. Don't try to wax a wet shirt; the wax won't penetrate well.

Having painted the leaves with green dye, Summers brushes on wax to protect them before immersing the fabric in the red dye bath.

9. Continue dyeing and waxing until you achieve the results you want.

Overdyeing the fabric to achieve the red hues.

10. Most of the wax can be removed by first flaking off all the wax you can and then ironing or boiling the shirt.

The finished St. Francis batik.

IRONING

Place the shirt between layers of newspaper and apply the iron, using a cotton setting. Replace the wet, waxy paper with fresh layers until most of the wax is absorbed. Remove the paper while the wax is still liquid so that the paper doesn't stick to the shirt. Professionally dry-clean the shirt.

BOILING

Immerse the shirt in boiling water for three to four minutes. Take it out carefully and sub-merge it in cold water. If it's still waxy, either boil it again (this time in soapy water) or take it to a dry cleaner you trust.

*For the three gorgeous batik shirts appearing here and on pages 122 and 134, artist **George Summers, Jr.** used discharge dyeing as part of the batik process. First, he dyed each shirt a dark color. Then using melted wax, he drew in the designs, using a tjanting for fine lines and a hard bristle brush for the heavier work. He then placed the T-shirts in a bath of diluted bleach for a few moments. Next, he immersed them in a diluted white vinegar bath to neutralize the bleach and strip away the remaining color, leaving just the waxed drawing. Summers thoroughly rinsed the shirts in cold water and let them dry. Last, he added color to each shirt using the traditional batik process of overdyeing from the lightest color to the darkest, using wax as the resist.*

The traditional "crackle" of batik shows up handsomely on this shirt by **Helen Suits**. She first outlined the fish and the surrounding background with a tjanting, using a mixture of paraffin and beeswax, for a medium crackle. Using brushes and thickened fiber-reactive dyes, she painted the fish aquamarine green and their fins yellow. She then brushed wax over the entire design, except for the inside of the fins, and flicked the brush a few times to produce bubbles. After the wax had cooled, she crumpled the shirt gently, forming hairline cracks for the dye to seep through. Mixing fuchsia and midnight blue dyes gave her a rich plum color, in which she immersed the entire shirt. The plum turned the unwaxed parts of the fins a medium brown.

Diana Light combined painting and overdying to imitate block printing—and create a colorful group of birds. First, she made a paper guide to mark the location of each square and the spaces in between. She centered the guide on the shirt, and used a water-soluble marker to transfer it. Then, she used the same marker to trace around a bird template in each square. She inserted a plastic-wrapped paper form inside the shirt, and applied a protective border of wax around the squares, about 2 inches (5 cm) wide. Next, she outlined the squares with the tjanting, then filled in with a brush, covering the 1/2-inch (1.3 cm) space between the squares, too. With the tjanting, she filled in each bird shape, but left the line of each bird's wing and eye unwaxed.

She brushed each square with a different dye color, left them to dry completely overnight, then boiled the shirt to remove the wax. The next day, she waxed over the squares once more, adding a narrow border around each, and carefully turned the shirt inside out (taking care not to crack the wax) and waxed the backs of the squares, too (to prevent excess dye from bleeding through to the front of the design). Finally, she overdyed the shirt with black.

This mysterious T-shirt, designed by **George Summers, Jr.** was done using a traditional batik process. He drew the design with wax and a tjanting, and then applied the color, overdyeing from light to dark.

The inspiration for the design comes from Summers' affinity for "masked cultures" and for holidays such as Halloween, Mardi Gras, and Carnival, where a bacchanal rite of passage takes place, usually before holy days. It is also the artist's interpretation of how, as humans, we all wear masks to cover our fears and shortcomings, and how special it is when people lift the mask to reveal who they really are.

Batik

Batik allows a designer to produce strikingly detailed work. After **Helen Suits** used a tjanting to draw an oriental woman's face, she painted the lips and a flower red, waxed over both, and dyed the shirt a deep, rich black.

A one-color batik is a good starting project—for example, outlining a cat and some former fish with tjanting and brush, dyeing the shirt red, and removing the wax. The rear half of this hungry feline stretches over the shoulder and down the back of the shirt.

Batik

This T-shirt was inspired by William Shakespeare's play, *A Midsummer Night's Dream*. The Pan figure, god of fields, forests, and shepherd's flocks, is often represented with a human face and torso, and the horns and legs of a goat. **George Summers, Jr.** wanted the front of the shirt to suggest merriment and revelry.

The quotes on the back, also by the famous bard, complete the mood. Summers' batik technique is described on page 127.

Batik

On a short shirt, **Shiila Carson** painted a rainbow of fiber reactive dyes—fuchsia, purple, and turquoise—then repeated the sequence diagonally down one side. Departing from normal practice, Carson didn't place a protective layer inside the shirt to prevent paint from staining the back. Instead, she allowed it to bleed through, then followed those lines when painting the back to match the front. When the dyes were dry she waxed over them, using paraffin for a heavy crackle, then dyed the shirt black.

Timothy Putney outlined his whale medallion with a tjanting, and waxed other areas to remain white. Then, working from light to dark, he applied robin's egg blue with a sponge brush, covering parts of the water and the entire whale, and painted the mountains light gray. He waxed the areas he wanted to remain those colors, and proceeded to add, then wax, other colors: turquoise, azure, navy blue, and green to the water, dark gray and black to the mountains. After waxing the finished medallion, he tied the shirt with string and dyed it blue.

Batik

Tracy Sanders begins her batik on a white T-shirt that has been washed with a mild dish-washing soap to remove the fabric finish. Using a tjanting, she draws the design on the shirt with a 50/50 mixture of beeswax and paraffin. Using primary colors, she mixes the thickened dye in small batches, and applies each color with a brush to color in the design. After the dye dries, she waxes over the design using a paintbrush, adding additional design elements with the tjanting. Now she is ready to dye the background color. Sanders uses a sink and fiber reactive vat dyes, following the manufacturer's directions for thickening.

Funky Dancers began when Sanders drew a simple square on the shirt. Next she sketched in the dancers and other shapes with her tjanting. Her last step was to color in the design with dyes.

Designer **Tracy Sanders'** rendering of a steaming cup of coffee looks good enough to drink. The rainbow of colors behind the cup complements the happy mood of the image. A description of how she batiks her shirts appears on page 138.

Batik

A giraffe's neck is the most elongated line a designer ever gets. **Helen Suits** outlined the animal with a tjanting and drew a flower for it to nibble on, then waxed the larger areas with a brush. She painted the bloom with thickened lilac and teal dyes, waxed over the flower, and mixed black and yellow dyes for the rest of the shirt.

Bright green dye and a broad brush were **Shiila Carson's** primary tools for this dressy shirt. She waxed half of it with paraffin, for extensive crackle. After the wax dried, she applied a second coat along the edge of the waxed area, so she'd get a less crackled stripe along the diagonal line. Then she crumpled and dyed the shirt.

141

Batik

This effervescent fish motif, designed by **Tracy Sanders**, is a good example of the importance of a well-balanced composition. Her batik process is described on page 138.

We couldn't resist including a silk T-shirt in this collection. **Marilyn Forth** used resist and fiber reactive dyes to transform a white crepe de Chine shirt into a magnificent blooming garden.

First she inserted a plastic-wrapped paper form inside the shirt to stretch the fabric and prevent the dye from bleeding through to the back. Next, she taped the shirt to her covered work table so that it wouldn't slide around. She sketched her design on the shirt with chalk pencil; then she drew on top of those lines with a tjanting and beeswax. She hand painted the flowers with dye. When the front was dry, she brushed navy dye on the back, being sure to overlap the brush strokes on all the solid areas. She mopped up any excess dye with paper towels to prevent uneven coloration. When the shirt was dry, she steamed it following the dye manufacturer's instructions. After washing the silk T with a mild dish washing soap and plenty of water, she ironed it dry on a clean sheet and then had it professionally dry-cleaned.

Batik

Fleta Monaghan produced an interesting variation of the Stars and Stripes for this shirt. First she stretched it on a cardboard frame, then she painted some pink stars and the red stripes of the flag, using thickened dyes. She waxed the painted parts and the areas she wanted to remain white: a few stars on the sleeves, and the rest of the flag. Then, using a blunt tapestry needle, she scratched thin lines in the wax: stars in the upper left corner of the flag; arrows, lines, and words on the rest. (This scratching technique is known as sgraffito.) Finally, she dyed the shirt a rich purple, using a mixture of fuchsia, turquoise, and navy dyes.

Early Mexican drawings inspired this shirt. **Fleta Monaghan** first sketched the figures on the shirt in soft lead pencil, then went over the lines with a tjanting. She painted the figures in thickened lilac dye, then painted their eyes and the nearby doors in yellow. Once they were dry, she waxed the painted areas and scratched details in the wax with a blunt needle. She brushed navy dye over the figures (thus dyeing the scratched details) and around the figures themselves. Then she improvised. She painted the rest of the shirt in maroon, waxed the figures and some of the maroon areas, and painted on deep brown dye. After she had boiled off the wax, she longed for deeper, richer color in places, so she overpainted a few areas in black.

Batik

To produce a lush rain forest, **Fleta Monaghan** painted layer upon layer of dye, waxing a few more areas each time. First she drew her design in soft lead pencil, then outlined vines, leaves, and fruit with a tjanting. She painted yellow and turquoise inside the vines and leaves, and orange in the fruit. Next she waxed the parts of vine and leaf that she wanted to remain yellow and blue, then painted the whole shirt bright green. Still restless, she added dark red accents to the fruit, waxed the areas in the leaves and vines she wanted to remain true green, and painted over the whole shirt in dark forest green.

If the year's first snowfall moves you to frolic, you'll understand this shirt. **Fleta Monaghan** painted some dancing figures in purple, waxed over them, and drew mountain shapes with a tjanting and brush. She also dropped splotches of wax on the sky, for snowflakes, and drew a moon and comet. With those dry, she painted turquoise on the sky and yellow on the mountains, then waxed stars, a moon, and more hills. To finish off, she painted violet dye on the sky and true green on the mountains, waxed again, then added navy blue to the sky and dark green to the mountains.

Batik

A variety of techniques appear on this shirt. **Ellen Zahorec** penciled a design on a plywood block and traced over it with white glue. When the glue was tacky, she pressed string into it, to create a raised, three dimensional pattern. Instead of dipping the string in fabric paint and stamping it on the fabric—a common technique—Zahorec dipped the block in a liquid resist available in some craft stores. She then stamped the pattern on a shirt and dyed it brown, leaving zigzagged patterns undyed. She overdyed until she liked the color, then painted an Indian-style totem pole down the center, using acrylic concentrates and dimensional paint.

A commercial bottled resist helped to produce this shirt in varying shades of purple. **Ellen Zahorec** dyed the shirt a dark lavender, then spread resist over the center of the shirt and overdyed again, darkening the remainder of the shirt. She then painted designs in acrylic and dimensional paints.

Marbling

Resembling the stone for which the process was named, marbling is a magical way to apply paint to a T-shirt. Swirls and eddies of color make each marbled shirt unique. The results are achieved by laying fabric paints on the surface of a specially thickened bath and swirling and combing them into patterns. The shirt, placed on top of the patterned colors, picks up a mirror image of the paint.

Preparing the Shirt

The first step is to treat the shirt with a mordant, a chemical that combines with fabric paint and dye to form an insoluable compound, the result being that the paint or dye adheres to the fabric. In a plastic bucket, soak a clean white or light- to medium-colored shirt in a solution of ⅓ cup (65 g) aluminum sulfate crystals—also known as alum—to a gallon (3.785 l) of cool tap water for about 30 minutes. One cup (200 g) of alum dissolved in 3 gallons of water (11.355 l) will mordant about 25 shirts!

If you are preparing more than one T-shirt, place only one at a time into the alum water, and use a stick or plastic implement to submerge the shirt in the solution. Protect your hands with latex gloves (alum water is used to make pickles: it dries the skin) and

pull the shirt from the solution. Roll it into a meatloaf-shaped bundle, and twist it over the bucket until the excess alum is squeezed out. Inspect the shirt for any dry spots; alum doesn't penetrate as readily as plain water. If necessary, soak and wring out the shirt again. Use the spin cycle in your washing machine (no rinse, just spin), or dry the shirt on a clothesline or drying rack. Avoid breathing the alum dust or dripping the alum solution on your skin, clothing, or nice wood floor. It is mildly acidic, like vinegar.

To make the shirt easier to handle in the bath and prevent paint from bleeding from the front to the back, you need to stretch it flat over some kind of form. One approach is to cut a form from corrugated cardboard. For ease of fit, cut the cardboard in two overlapping halves, each about three-fifths the total width of the torso. Add about 2 inches (5 cm) all around the shirt to make it easier to grip. Before inserting the cardboard into the shirt, crush the outer edges to form a mock-beveled edge; then cover these edges with masking tape. The compressed edges will minimize the white line between the front and back of the printed image. Cover the two cardboard pieces with plastic wrap and slip them inside the shirt. Position them so that the fabric is taut; then tape the halves together.

*To create this jazzy shirt, left, designer **Carl Weis** laid down bright colors in a large "V" design, front and back. Then, using a single stylus, he made a few quick strokes, some radiating to and from the neck and others in and out from the center.*

Marbling

Making a Tray for the Bath

You will need a waterproof, rectangular tray, at least 2 to 3 inches deep (5 to 7.5 cm) and long and wide enough to hold a flat T-shirt.

*This is the back of the shirt shown on page 150. Designer **Carl Weis** swirled the paint in the the center to complement the floral motif on the front.*

Professional T-shirt marblers make a tray that measures 3½ feet wide (1.2 m) by 7 feet long (2 m). A 4-by-8 foot (1.2 by 2.5 m) sheet of ⅝-inch (1.5 cm) or ¾-inch (2 cm) plywood makes an excellent base when positioned at table height. With a tray this large, you can create a pattern for the front of the shirt at one end of the tray and a matching or different pattern at the other end of the tray for the back of the shirt.

After you marble the front, you carefully flip the shirt over and marble the back at the other end of the tray.

To make a smaller tray, you can use 1-by-4-inch (2.5 by 10 cm) lumber, cut to appropriate lengths for the sides, held by small nails or even duct tape. Line the tray with a double layer of 3 ml clear, plastic shower liner, tucked down into the corners. Before lining the tray with plastic, insert a piece of paper outlined with the shape of the front of a stretched-flat T-shirt (for a larger tray, insert an outlined piece for the back of the shirt, too). This way, you will know where to put the colors on the water to create the patterns you want.

The Bath Fluid or Size

The bath fluid or size is water thickened with cellulose to the consistency of gelatin that is just starting to set. The thickener, methyl cellulose or hydroxyethyl cellulose, is a white powder that is an extract of wood pulp.

To make a small batch of size, vigorously stir 4 tablespoons (15 g) of methyl cel into 1 gallon (3.785 l) of warm tap water for two to three minutes. Then add 2 tablespoons (29.6 ml) of clear household ammonia, and stir until the mixture looks clear—about two minutes. Let this set for 30 minutes, stirring it now and then to test the thickness—it should be slick like egg white. Finally, add 2 teaspoons (9.8 ml) of white vinegar to neutralize the pH, and stir again for two minutes. Pour the size into the marbling tray and let it stand for about 12 hours. You will need a bath fluid that is about 2 inches (5 cm) deep. For a larger tray, multiply the recipe accordingly.

One professional marbler uses this recipe to fill his 3½-feet-wide (1.2 m) by 7-feet-long (2 m) tray:

- 10 to 11 gallons (38 to 42 l) of cold tap water

- 2½ cups (500 g) of methyl cel or hydroxyethyl cellulose

- 2 fluid ounces (59 ml) of ammonia

- 2 fluid ounces (59 ml) of vinegar.

This 8 gallon (30 l) mixture is enough to marble about 25 shirts. The marbler adds another gallon or two after the first few shirts are marbled.

Marbling Tools

You can create a beautiful marbled pattern simply in the way you throw the paint onto the size. You can also create a variety of traditional and unique patterns using a few simple tools that you can easily make with available materials.

For free-form patterns or drawn images, a stylus is essential. It can be any object with a single long point, such as a chopstick, a rattail comb, a twig, a bamboo skewer, or a knitting needle. To use a stylus, hold it vertically and insert the tip in the bath. As you move it around, the paint will swirl into patterns.

Many patterns can be made by combing the paint. A comb can be an ordinary hair comb, or you can make your own. To do this, cut a piece of corrugated cardboard or foam core 1 inch wide (2.5 cm) and as long as your tray is wide. Stick straight pins into one long edge at ½ inch (1.5 cm) intervals. To make a rake, insert the pins 1 inch (2.5 cm) apart.

A *bouquet comb* can be made by cutting a piece of cardboard 2 inches (5 cm) wide, and inserting two rows of pins through its flat surface; each row should be ½ inch (1.5 cm) in from a long edge. Space the pins 2 inches (5 cm) apart so that they are not directly across from each other.

Raking, combing, and drawing are usually done across the grain of existing color patterns.

The Paints

All you need now are acrylic fabric paints sold at any craft-supply store. Thin them with water to the consistency of light cream. You can pour them into narrow-tipped plastic bottles; turkey basters and large medicine droppers make good delivery vehicles. About 2 to 3 fluid ounces (59 to 89 ml) of paint is enough for the typical overall color pattern, front and back. A broom corn or nylon whisk can deliver smaller droplets of color, if desired.

Patterns

T-shirt marblers tend to be an experimental bunch who enjoy free-form designing. There are no hard and fast rules to marbling, so just have fun and experiment. If you'd rather follow a pattern, here are a few to choose from.

Marbling

Top Left: Get Gel
Top Right: Zebra
Bottom Left: Bouquet
Bottom Right: Nonpareil

GET GEL

1. Cover the surface of the size with dots of paint.

2. Rake across the tray, from left to right.

3. Rake back across the tray, from right to left. On this second pass, put the teeth halfway between the lines you made on the first pass.

4. Rake down the length of the tray.

5. Rake back up the length of the tray. This is a vertical get gel—the lines will end up going up and down—which will look good on a T-shirt. To make a horizontal get gel, first rake up and down the length of the tray, then rake back and forth.

ZEBRA

1. Make a get gel.

2. Drop droplets of paint over the pattern.

NONPAREIL

1. Make a horizontal get gel.

2. Comb straight down the length of the tray.

BOUQUET

1. Make a nonpareil.

2. Bring the bouquet comb down the length of the tray, moving the tool in a wavy, zigzag motion.

Step By Step

After you've mordanted the T-shirt, stretched it on a cardboard form, and filled the tray with size, the real magic begins.

1. Skim the size by dragging a strip of newspaper over the surface of the bath.

2. Pattern-making starts with how the colors are laid down—circles, spirals, chevrons, lines, dots—whatever moves you at the moment. Use an eyedropper or narrow-tipped bottle to drop dots of paint on the surface of the size. The dots should spread so they are 2 to 3 inches (5 to 7.5 cm) wide. If the paint sinks, add more water to the paint mixture; if the drops spread too much, add more paint. Paints do have a preferred order—white and black need to be laid down early or they will sink. Each brand and color has its own chemistry—there is no substitute for experimentation and experience! (A very dilute solution of dish detergent can be added to colors that chronically sink. Used by itself, it can clear an area of color to create a dramatic effect or make room for a screen-printed image.)

3. Continue to add paint, using additional colors, until the surface of the size is covered to your satisfaction.

4. Use the marbling tools to swirl the paint into patterns. Dip the teeth of a comb into the size and carefully move the tool back and forth.

5. Take the stretched flat shirt (ideally, still slightly damp with alum, as this picks up and holds color better than a bone-dry shirt) and carefully lay it down, front first, onto the bath. With dry fingers, gently tap the back of the shirt to release any tiny air bubbles that may be trapped between the shirt and the size; they will prevent the paint from evenly penetrating the fabric. After a minute or two, you are ready to lift up the shirt.

This is the moment of greatest anticipation and potential mishap. Keep the shirt as level as possible when you lift it (there will be suction at work), and hold it in place for a few second to drain. Take a breath, exhale, and in one fluid motion, flip the shirt over with your arms extended in front of you. If your tray is large enough to hold the paint pattern for the back, simply lay the shirt down again and print the back. If you need to lay down more paint, set the shirt aside on clean plastic sheeting, skim the tray, and make another pattern like the first one or a modification of it; then marble the back of the shirt. You can tap the shirt with wet fingers this time. Allow 10 seconds for the colors to set before picking up the shirt again. You may want to invite a friend to help you flip the shirt.

6. Hold the now slimy shirt by the armpits, and let it drain just inside the edge of the bath for about 20 to 30 seconds. Rotate it 180 degrees and carry it quickly to a nearby sink, bathtub, or the backyard, where you can rinse the shirt front and back with a gentle spray from a garden hose or other type of sprayer. Keep the nozzle moving, so that you can deliver water quickly all over the shirt, starting where the stretcher shows at the neck; then return as needed to areas where the paint may be bleeding. Spot rinse again after 30 minutes, if any colors seem to have run. Let the shirt drain for several hours to an entire day, then unstretch it while it is slightly damp. This is the time to touch up the edges of the shirt that may not be adequately marbled by using matching paint and a brush. You can paint the damp shirt while it is on or off the stretcher.

7. Air-dry the shirt thoroughly. Test the hem and the neck. Heat set the paint by placing the shirt in a clothes dryer on a high setting for 8 to 10 minutes. Do not overcook! (Unreacted alum can later eat holes in the fabric; 20 minutes of heat may result in beautiful rags!)

8. Give the shirt a final rinse by hand or in your washing machine on the delicate cycle (no soap, warm/cold water). Line- or machine-dry your finished marbled shirt.

Marbled fabric resembles the stone for which the process was named. There are swirls and eddies of color, and no two shirts turn out exactly alike. Rather than using acrylic fabric paints and methyl cellulose size, **Sandra Holzman** floated oil-based silk-screen inks for textiles on a tray of plain water and swirled them into fluid patterns to produce this motion-filled shirt.

Marbling

To create her American flag motif, appropriately named *Stars and Stripes*, **Kristen Day** placed blue and red paint on the bath and combed these colors to achieve an animated, breezy effect. Then she placed adhesive-backed stars on the shirt as a *frisket*, or masking device, before laying the shirt on the bath surface.

The mood of **Geoffrey Scott-Alexander's** piece has a great deal to do with his selection of complementary, rich colors. After laying down the paint, he used a minimum of strokes with a small nonpareil comb to create tails and trails that yield serene, yet vital movement to the pattern. The finished design is evocative of music, dance, or the space of a dream.

Marbling

Marbled fabrics manage to look delicate even when the colors are bright. **Sandra Holzman** used rust, bright yellow, beige, and brown textile paints to produce a striking, all-over design.

Unlike the shirt on the previous page, this one has a traditional, structured pattern. Using acrylic fabric paints and a methyl cel size, **Mimi Schleicher** made a horizontal get gel (see page 154) using light blue, dark blue, violet, green, and black. To make the fleurs-de-lis, she added paint a drop at a time, one drop inside the other, to make bull's-eyes: dark blue, light blue inside that, then dark blue again. Then she used a stylus to pull the bull's-eyes into the shapes she wanted.

Marbling

This magical bird emerged when **Carl Weis**, having made a horizontal pattern with a bouquet rake (double row of teeth spaced 3 inches/7.5 cm apart), made a sweeping upward stroke with a non-pareil comb (teeth equally spaced about $\frac{5}{8}$ inch/1.5 cm apart). He then formed the head and bill by stroking a single stylus several times through the existing patterns. The eye, which he applied last, was a single drop of color. Weis named this shirt—one of his favorites—*Dance of Summer*.

Marbler **Carl Weis** has blended his art with a screened image of two polar bears by David Wenzel, ©1994 Jim Morris Environmental T-Shirt Company. Weis first threw down the color, and then cleared it in the screened area, using a paint dispersant. The result is a truly handsome shirt with arctic colors and patterns that conjure up the wintry conditions these animals so enjoy.

Marbling

Blocks of marbling are as interesting as an all-over pattern. **Mimi Schleicher** cut a shirt-sized stencil from freezer paper, snipping away various four-sided shapes, and ironed the stencil to the shirt. (The shiny side adhered to the fabric.) She then made a zebra pattern (see page 154) on her marbling tray in red, cranberry, russet, violet, black, yellow, and white. When she laid the shirt on top, it was marbled only in the empty spaces.

This subtle shirt relies on an ancient design— the triangle—and a centuries-old pattern of marbling, known as nonpareil. **Mimi Schleicher** ironed a stencil cut from freezer wrap onto an off-white shirt; made a nonpareil of green, dark green, pewter green, russet, yellow, and black; and created a handsome T-shirt.

Marbling

Lisa Shelton achieved the fluorescent veins of color in this crop-top by first laying down a stone pattern with bright-colored paints. Then she added white drops of paint that spread, pushing the fluorescent colors together to create a vibrant effect.

Lori Sylvester used turkey basters to deposit her intense colors in separate areas on the bath fluid. Her directional combing and stylus work impart a distinctive energy to the finished piece.

Marbling

Most marblers are incapable of throwing away even the smallest scrap of marbled fabric. **Laura Sims** found yet another way to use the leftovers. She drew a tropical fish pattern, found some remarkably fishlike fabric, and bought some iron-on bonding web (normally used to make a fast hem). She cut out a fabric fish and a web fish, laid the former on the latter, and ironed both onto a black T-shirt. Using the same technique, she added marine plants and a fishy companion. To finish, she outlined the shapes in black dimensional paint and dotted in a few magenta bubbles, also with dimensional paint.

Craft stores sell books of copyright-free designs, specifically designed for the craftsperson in search of ideas. **Laura Sims** found this oriental knot in just such a source. She traced it onto a piece of marbled fabric with a washable pen, cut out the fabric and a matching piece of iron-on bonding web, and ironed the design onto the shirt. To finish the edges, she outlined the design with black dimensional paint.

Marbling

Thom Bruni used a special hinged Butterfly™ comb to create dramatic effects, otherwise impossible to achieve. He laid down the colors and made a few short strokes with a stylus to give them interest. Then he added drops of yellow and bright green and pulled the paints with a stylus. Is this an owl's face or that of another, wilder, creature?

Babies and toddlers look wonderful in marbled clothes, such as this lovely romper, marbled by **Lisa Shelton**. The black and white paint she added to the blue and yellow adds dimension to the marbling. She achieved the simple drip pattern by pulling her rake down through the paint.

Marbling

This child-size shirt has a bouquet pattern, created with a traditional bouquet comb. **Mimi Schleicher** cut a pair of hearts from a sheet of freezer wrap and ironed the stencil onto the shirt. Her bouquet includes red, yellow, cranberry, violet, and black.

Less than perfect shirts can often be rescued. When the pink and blue marbling in the middle turned out rather drab, **Ellen Zahorec** livened it up. She outlined the bouquet pattern in black dimensional paint, and drew some three-petaled flowers around the border, which she painted in acrylic fabric paint. Some neon green leaves woke up the whole design.

Screenprinting & Transferring

Screenprinting is merely an advanced form of stenciling. A simple frame over which polyester screen fabric (once upon a time it was silk) is stretched and a rubber squeegee make up the printing press. Using one of several methods, you create a stencil to mask or block out portions of the screen. Then you use the squeegee to force paint through the unmasked areas and onto the shirt.

Screen Frame

You can purchase inexpensive screen frames and screen fabric in good craft and art-supply stores or in mail-order catalogs. Or you can make your own. Construct a simple wooden square or rectangular frame and miter the corners if you want, joining them with corrugated fasteners sold at hardware stores. To add strength to the frame, glue the corners together with wood glue. One designer makes a very useable screen by stapling the polyester mesh to four artist's stretcher strips.

Cut a piece of polyester screen fabric 2 inches (5 cm) longer and wider than the frame. When you attach the screen to the frame using a staple gun, you need to stretch the mesh as tightly as possible. Staple the center of one side and, pulling directly across, staple the opposite center. After stapling the other two centers, work toward the corners, pulling and stapling as you go.

You may want to mask the edges of the screen so paint can't seep out and around it and stain the fabric. The gummed paper tape used to wrap packages for mailing works well. Tape around the mesh on the outside of the frame. Then tape around the inside edges, folding the tape in half lengthwise so that half of the strip is on the mesh and half is up the side of the frame. Finally, shellac over the tape, inside and out.

Squeegee

A squeegee consists of a strip of hard, rubbery material attached to a handle. You can purchase inexpensive ones in craft and art-supply stores and mail-order catalogs. You can also improvise with a piece of foam core or dull-edged acrylic. Make your own by sandwiching a piece of firm weatherstripping between two pieces of fiberboard. Other objects work, too, such as plastic spatulas and old credit cards.

Scotty and ***Tracey Tardiff*** *created the shirts that appear on pages 176, 178, and 182. Details appear on page 182. All the imagery in their screenprinted shirts reflects the natural world and the cycle of life. The shirt at the left, which they call* Harmonized Dancing, *depicts beings embracing the warmth of the sun and, on the back, the glow of the moon.*

Whatever tool you use, be sure the paint or dye evenly covers the image on the shirt. It helps to force the paint or dye through the screen by moving the squeegee or plastic edge from the top of the screen to the bottom, then from one side to the other, then from the bottom to the top, etc.

Paints and Dyes

You can use most textile paints, acrylic paints, and thickened fiber reactive dyes for screen printing. There are also textile inks designed just for this purpose. Follow the manufacturer's directions for each product. Thick paint is one of the secrets to successful screen printing. It needs to be thick in order to be squeezed through the fine mesh of the screen and onto the shirt. Thin paints or dyes will drip through the screen and print inadequately and unevenly.

Paper Stencils

Although they do not last very long, paper stencils are by far the easiest stencils to make. If you are making only one shirt, you may want to use a paper stencil. This is also a good place to start if you are new to screen printing. Paper stencils lend themselves well to large lettering and simple shapes.

SHIRT STENCILS

If the paper will adhere to the shirt and if you want to print the stencil just one time on the shirt, you can simply lay the screen on top of the stencil on the shirt and squeegee the paint directly across it. Try masking tape for blocking out straight borders and geometric shapes. Or, cut freezer wrap into desired shapes and iron them onto the T-shirt.

SCREEN STENCILS

If you plan to print the design on the shirt more than once or print more than one shirt, the paper stencil needs to stick to the screen. The first step is to cut out the stencil. Various kinds of paper will work, including butcher, good-quality bond, and waxed stenciling paper. Place the stencil on a piece of scrap fabric, put the screen on top (mesh side down), and squeegee paint across the surface. The paint will adhere the stencil to the screen.

Lacquer Film Stencils

These stencils last much longer than paper ones, are easy to cut, and work well for cutting intricate designs with sharp, clear lines. Lacquer film consists of a very thin layer of lacquer, temporarily laminated with rubber cement to a transparent paper or plastic backing. The backing sheet holds the cut stencil elements in place until the cut film is adhered to the screen; then the backing sheet is stripped from the screen.

STEP BY STEP

1. Draw the design on paper, making sure it fits inside your screen frame. Leave about 2 inches (5 cm) of space at the top and bottom, and an extra inch (2.5 cm) along each side of the frame. You will need this additional room so the squeegeed paint has some place to start and finish.

2. Place the drawing face up on a hard surface and tape down the corners. Lay the lacquer film—film side up—on top of the drawing, and tape it down, as well. (Tip: The lacquer film with a plastic backing is much easier to use.)

3. Use a craft knife to cut out the design, being sure to cut *only through the lacquer layer,* not through the backing. Cut away areas you want to print; the paint will be blocked out wherever the lacquer film remains. Carefully lift off the cutout areas of lacquer film; what remains will become the stencil.

4. To adhere the lacquer stencil to the screen, place it, lacquer side up, on a stack of newspaper, and place the screen on top, with the mesh facing down, so that it almost touches the lacquer. Wet a rag with solvent (lacquer thinner), and rub it into the center of the screen, using a circular motion to soften the lacquer. Complete a small area of the stencil, and rub it again with a clean, dry rag, pressing down firmly. This pressure will force the softened lacquer into the screen mesh and create the stencil. Working outward from the center, continue to bond the stencil to the screen.

5. Allow the screen to dry; then peel off the backing. If a part of the lacquer sticks to the backing rather than to the screen, repeat the thinning and adhering process for that area. (Tip: Do *not* buy water-soluble film designed for screen printing with solvent-based inks. Although it is very easy to use, the stencil will dissolve if you use water-based textile paints.)

Photo Emulsion Stencils

An increasingly popular method of creating stencils for screen printing, photo emulsion stencils are fun and easy to make. Screen emulsion is a thick liquid that hardens when exposed to ultraviolet light—either direct sunlight or a light box. Basically, you coat your screen with emulsion, place a flat, light-blocking image—called the "photo positive"—on the screen, and "burn" the screen with ultraviolet light. The emulsion exposed to the light becomes hard; the emulsion blocked from

Screenprinting & Transferring

the light by the photo positive is rinsed away with water. You are left with an open area of design on your screen that will print on your T-shirt.

*This is the back of the shirt shown on page 174 by **Scotty** and **Tracey Tardiff**.*

PHOTO POSITIVE

Anything flat that will block out light can be a photo positive: a leaf, a paper doily, cut-paper stars, paper letters. You can press self-adhesive letters (or other shapes) onto clear acetate. The letters will block the light, the acetate will not, and you will end up with a lettered stencil. Or you can trace a design onto clear acetate and fill it in with very dense, black ink so that the ultraviolet light cannot penetrate the image.

You can make a photo positive image from special ruby-colored film that blocks ultraviolet light and is laminated to a clear plastic backing. When you cut away the red film from the areas you don't want to print, you will wind up with a photo positive. As with lacquer film, be careful not to cut through the clear backing.

There are two other ways you can create a photo positive. Most copy machines will copy an image onto clear acetate. This means you can copy a high-contrast black-and-white photo onto acetate and end up with a black-and-clear sheet that you can place on your emulsion-coated screen. You can achieve a similar result in a darkroom. A photo shop can make a film positive for you, a transparency of a black-and-white print—in effect, a sheet of clear film with opaque black areas.

STEP BY STEP

1. Work in dim light; a yellow light bulb works fine, as does an incandescent light at the other end of the room. You don't need to invest in a red light, such as those used in photo darkrooms. Avoid working in fluorescent light or sunlight, which will expose your image before you're ready. Apply a thin coat of emulsion to the screen, using a squeegee to spread it evenly. Make sure the entire surface of the screen, inside and out, is coated. Let the screen dry in the dark overnight.

2. In dim light again, place the dry screen on a padded board. Position the photo positive on the central area of the reverse side of your screen (the image should appear backwards on the back side of the screen).

3. In order to get a tight contact between the screen and the photo positive, place a piece of wood or a thin book on the inside of the screen to provide a smooth, flat resting surface for the image. Then place the piece of glass or plastic sheet on top.

4. If you plan to use solar exposure, cover the assembled screen and photo positive "sandwich" with a blanket and carry it outside to a sunny area. (Don't attempt solar exposures on an overcast day.) Place it on a table and remove the blanket. Exposure times will vary depending on the light source and the thickness of the emulsion coating, but three to five minutes is generally adequate for direct sunlight or a good lightbox. Replace the blanket and carry the materials back inside to dim light.

5. Remove the glass or plastic sheet, and gently spray the screen with cool or lukewarm water for about five minutes to wash the emulsion off the unexposed areas.

6. Blot off the excess water, and let the screen dry overnight. Now you are ready to use a squeegee to force paint, dye, or ink through the open-mesh image area of the screen.

PHOTO SENSITIVE SCREEN

Another approach is to call a T-shirt print company in your area that does screen printing (that's what most do), and ask them to make you a *photo sensitive screen* from your black-and-white drawing. It doesn't cost very much and is especially good for lettering and images with fine details. Then you use that screen for printing on your shirt.

Image Transfers

Transfer papers now offer a fun alternative to screenprinting. Any image 11 x 17 inches (27.9 x 43.2 cm) or smaller can be copied onto transfer paper designed for use with fabric, then ironed in place on a T-shirt. Craft and office supply-stores sell the transfer papers, and many copy centers even stock them. Some of the papers are known as "wet-release" transfer papers, which simply means that after you iron on your image, you have to sponge water on the transfer paper's backing to release it and reveal the image. Other papers are made for use with ink-jet printers, so you can print scanned or other computerized images directly onto the paper (think digitally manipulated photos or computer clip art). A white or light colored shirt in a cotton/poly blend works best for fabric transfers. In most cases, you can machine wash a T-shirt featuring an image transfer if you turn it inside out and launder it using a delicate cycle. Dry it flat or on a line for best results.

Cutaway view of leaves (the photo positive) positioned on the emulsion-coated screen, covered by a piece of glass

Screenprinting & Transferring

Designer **Ellen Zahorec** combined several techniques for this shirt. First, she made a lacquer film stencil, blocking out the birds, leaves, and decorative swirls. She screen printed the background, using a "split font" technique: with deep blue textile ink on the left side of the screen, burgundy in the center, and burnt orange on the right, she squeegeed them through the screen onto the shirt simultaneously. After the print dried, she used masking tape to block out the areas around the border and printed a purple frame for the design. Finally, she went back and painted in the negative areas of the stenciled design (the ones still white), using a brush and fabric paint: the brilliant plumage of the birds, the electric green leaves, and the exuberant swirls of color. She finished off the detail lines with a paint marker.

A friend sketched this saucy lady in a hat, and **Terry Taylor** knew right away she'd look smashing—decked out with earrings and a necklace—on the front of a T-shirt. He enlarged the drawing first, then copied it onto a piece of fabric transfer paper. Next, he simply followed the manufacturer's instructions for applying the image to the front of the shirt with a bit of ironing. Adding the perfect finishing panache was easy. He hand-stitched a resin bead on each ear and a smaller series of resin beads along the neckline.

This striking design, created by, **Scotty** and **Tracey Tardiff**, shows the continents dividing from Pangaea, the planetary spirits guiding the earth around the sun, and the birth of the moon. After cutting their designs in lacquer film, they used solar exposure to create the film positives for the screen print. On 100 percent cotton shirts, they applied semitransparent, water-based dyes that are fiber reactive. With a squeegee, they blend, layer, and splatter colors directly onto the screen to achieve different effects.

This attractive shirt, designed by **Amanda Kibler**, is called *Color Face*, a play on words that describes the different typefaces used. First, she cut the shapes for the pastel colors from lacquer film. She adhered the stencil to the blank screen and printed the shapes with pastel-colored textile inks. Then she allowed the shirt to dry thoroughly.

For the jumble of letters, she created a photo positive and placed it on top of the colored background. She printed the letters with black textile inks. As a finishing touch, she taped individual letters onto the shirt and printed them in a random pattern. She heat-set the shirt in her clothes dryer for 30 minutes. Then she ironed it on the wrong side with the iron on the cotton setting.

Screenprinting & Transferring

Hughes Family Reunion
July 25th at City Park

Annie Stromquist came up with this perfect party favor for a family reunion using two photo-emulsion stencils, each printed in a different color. For the first one, she selected a photograph featuring lots of contrasts; old black-and-white photos are perfect. She scanned the photo and enhanced the contrasts even more on her computer. (A staff member at a full-service copy center could also do this for you.) While she was at it, she enlarged the photo to the size she wanted for the shirt. For the second photo-emulsion stencil, she worked from computer-printed text (handwritten text would work just as well). She enlarged the text to a size that complemented the photo and would be easily readable from a short distance. She placed the stencils on an emulsion-coated screen, and printed each with a different textile screenprint ink. After the ink dried, she used a hot iron to seal the images.

school¹ (skŏŏl) n. Abbr. s., S., sch. 1. An institution for the instruction of children. 2. An institution for instruction in a skill or business. 3. A college or university. 4. An institution within a college or university for instruction in a specialized field. 5. The student body of an educational institution. 6. A place of instruction; the building or group of buildings in which instruction is given or in which students work and live. 7. The process of being educated; especially, formal education comprising a planned series of courses over a number of years. 8. A session of instruction. 9. A group of persons, especially intellectuals or artists, whose thought, work, or style demonstrates some common influence or unifying belief.

school² (skŏŏl) n. A large group of aquatic animals, especially fish, swimming together; a shoal. See Synonyms at flock. —intr.v. schooled, schooling, schools. To swim in, or form into, a school. [Middle English scole, from Middle Dutch schōle.] troop, group. See skel-¹ in Appendix.*]

school-boy (skŏŏl'boi') n. A boy attending school.

Snag this idea from **Dana Irwin**, and your search for the ideal graduation gift is over. She used fabric transfer paper to create this photographic retrospective celebrating her nephew's school years. After gathering his class pictures from first grade on, she sized them all on a color photocopier, reducing some and enlarging others, so they'd be similar in shape. She then cut them all out and glued them onto a sheet of white paper, positioning them in a loose grid. (Staggering is best, she says, so you don't have to worry about squaring up the design perfectly.) She copied the whole design onto transfer paper and had a copy shop press it onto a T-shirt. (You could also use iron-on transfer paper at home.) With the same paper, she transferred a clip-art image and a section from the dictionary defining "school" and "school boy."

Screenprinting & Transferring

A bright green shirt forms a fine backdrop for blue and purple mountains, complete with deer to roam in them. **Ellen Zahorec** ironed pieces of torn freezer paper onto the shirt to create the stencil for the craggy mountains, and applied masking tape to the shirt to make the design border and to block out geometric shapes. An old Christmas card with a cut-out reindeer supplied a ready-made stencil. Using transparent fabric inks, she printed multiple designs over each other in shades of magenta, purple, and blue. She then outlined various shapes with a black dry-eraser marker and painted a few stags with white acrylic fabric paint.

Screenprinting & Transferring

Lynne Caldwell used the happy fusion of nature and technology to create this vivid splash of color on the front of a crisp, white shirt. She started by snapping shots of a few sprigs of a leafy green plant with a digital camera, then printed out the photos, enlarged them on a color photocopier, and copied them onto a sheet of photo transfer paper. From the transfer paper, she cut out the pieces she wanted for her shirt, and ironed them on, following the transfer paper's packaging instructions. To add the splashes of fuchsia and lime, she cut leaf-shaped stencils in several sizes out of contact paper, and used fabric paint and a brush to add them around and on top of the photo transfer.

Screenprinting & Transferring

To create this design celebrating color and geometric shapes, **Amanda Kibler** first mixed textile inks in the colors she wanted. Then she drew the shapes on paper and assigned each a color. She cut out one lacquer film stencil and adhered it to the screen. Then she printed one color at a time, each time taping (with clear tape) those areas not to be printed. Instead of squeegees, Kibler used small spatulas to apply the ink. She let the shirt dry thoroughly. She rinsed the screen and removed the tape. On the dry screen, she taped off the motif elements to be printed and then printed. Finally, she added the tiny black dots with a brush and black ink. She heat set the shirt as described on page 183.

Susan Baylies designed this delightful Halloween shirt, a spooky marriage between screen printing and tie-dye. First, she crunched the presoaked shirt and placed it in the bottom of a dry bucket. She added purple cold water dye to clear water in another bucket. She added the activator, immediately poured the active dye water onto the T-shirt, and let it soak for one hour. Then she rinsed the shirt, washed it, and let it dry.

She made two silkscreens, one for the moon and one for the tree. Using her own photo enlarger, she turned a high-contrast black-and-white photo of a tree into a film positive. Last, she drew in all the other elements, using India ink and a brush.

Screenprinting & Transferring

Jean Penland used restraint and simplicity to create these two screen-printed shirts. First she made two drawings of bamboo stands (one is evident on the pocket of the white shirt; the other appears in the middle right of the black shirt). She had two photo sensitive screens made. Then she printed the designs with black and white acrylic paints. On the white shirt, she slipped a piece of cardboard in the pocket before printing. You could keep printing the two images across the shirt, or use the theory demonstrated here, that sometimes less is more.

Tip: When you use a screen to print an image more than one time, be sure to thoroughly wash the paint or dye from the screen, using warm water. Dry the screen with a hair dryer, and then print again.

Amanda **Kibler** calls this contemporary design *Dance*, and indeed, the two images give a colorful impression of two figures dancing. First, she cut stencils out of lacquer film—the black line outlines only—and adhered the stencil to the screen. She printed the black first, using black textile ink, and allowed it to dry. Then she placed mylar (you can use frosted or clear, medium- to heavyweight) on top of the black outlined shapes. She traced the shapes to be filled in with color, and then cut out the triangles, using a ruler and craft knife. She lightly sprayed the mylar with adhesive mount and placed the blank screen on top of the shapes to be painted. She printed the colored triangles with textile inks, applying the ink with two to three passes of the squeegee. As a last step, she heatset the shirt as described on page 183.

Screenprinting & Transferring

Forget the problem of missing the forest for the trees. **Lynne Caldwell** has come up with a leafy-green design that gives you both in one. She used a digital camera to photograph a wooded setting, then printed out her shots and chose one to enlarge on a color photocopier and print onto a sheet of photo transfer paper. From the transfer, she cut out a tree trunk and a variety of leaves, then followed the transfer paper's packaging instructions to iron them all onto the front of the shirt, arranging them in the shape of a tree. Using contact-paper stencils, she added a few fabric paint leaves to the mix, then outlined all the pieces with a green fabric marker to give the design some depth.

Remember the snowflakes you used to make in school by folding pieces of paper and cutting along the folds? **Ellen Zahorec** reclaimed that childhood technique for this shirt. She cut a snowflake out of freezer paper and laid it, shiny side up, on a piece of scrap muslin. She put the silk screen on top of the pattern and squeegeed transparent textile ink across the screen. The paper snowflake stuck to the back of the screen and could be used repeatedly on the shirt. She cut a similar stencil of a dancer and printed it across the top, overlapping the designs, and a triangular stencil for the center. Last, she added accents with fabric paint and paint pens.

Screenprinting & Transferring

Sandra Holzman began this luxurious shirt by dyeing it with fiber reactive dye, working in a bucket so that the color would be a bit uneven. She then cut two newsprint stencils—one for the squares, and one for the purple lines and triangles. She placed the first stencil on a piece of scrap fabric, set the screen frame on it, and squeegeed textile screen-printing ink across the screen, to adhere the stencil to the screen. She then printed the shirt, mixing blue and beige on the screen. After cleaning the screen, she adhered the lines-and-triangles stencil the same way and printed it in purple.

To get the image of a ballerina on a shirt, **Ellen Zahorec** xeroxed a black and white photo she found in a book on ballet. She took it to a photo store and had them create a photo transparency: black in the some areas, clear film in others. She coated her screen with emulsion, laid the photo transparency on top, and exposed it to sunlight, thus creating a stencil. She made a second photo stencil for the pinwheel designs, using a pattern from a book of geometric designs. Then she hand-painted the ballerina and outlined the pinwheel spokes in dimensional paint.

Screenprinting & Transferring

Dana Irwin created this elegant design without drawing a single line. She found the birds and the building in copyright-free books containing black and-white illustrations. She took the images to a photo shop where they were turned into three separate film positives, one for the black areas, one for the light gray areas, and one for the gradated yellow area. She placed each film positive on an emulsion-coated screen and printed the images with textile paints, being sure to paint the black images last.

These two charming birds, lightly stepping their way across a child-size T-shirt, are the inspiration of artist **Jean Penland**. She made two separate screens, one for each bird. Then she forced thick acrylic paint through the screen to print each bird. When the paint was dry, she overpainted the large bird's beak with silver paint, and filled in some of the unevenly painted areas with blue paint.

Screenprinting & Transferring

To make this triangular design, **Amanda Kibler** cut one lacquer film stencil and printed it with water-based fabric paints, using clear tape to block out those areas she didn't want to print with any given color. To get the marbled effect on the top diamonds and the large triangle at the bottom, she dropped small amounts of several colors directly onto the screen and made no more than two passes with the squeegee.

To get the background she wanted, **Sandra Holzman** dyed a white shirt with fiber reactive dye, using a bucket to get an uneven color. She then cut two newsprint stencils: one for the whimsical animals, and one for the stars. She adhered the first stencil to the back of the screen and printed several colors one by one, using different squeegees, until everything was printed. Then she printed the second stencil, using a similar technique.

Screenprinting & Transferring

M any people don't know this: craft stores sell eyes. Cheap. **Michelle Lipson** knows it, and she bought four pairs for her salamanders. First she cut the overall design from Rubylith and made a photo emulsion stencil, then she printed it in bright red. She added spots and strips with yellow dimensional paint, put the eyes in the right places, and adhered them to the shirt by circling them with the same sticky yellow paint. When the lizards roll their eyes, adults are unnerved; children are delighted.

A simple design can make an effective shirt. **Amanda Kibler** cut 16 squares from lacquer film and adhered the stencil to the screen. After assigning colors to squares, she printed one color at a time, each time taping out those blocks not to be printed with clear tape. She washed and dried the screen, and allowed the shirt to dry, after every color. Finally, she added accents with foam brushes and plastic pigment extruders.

Screenprinting & Transferring

JoAnn Giordano combined a simple hand-cut stencil—the gold leaves shown on the shirt—and a photo emulsion screen print to produce this striking image of Mexican painter Frida Kahlo. First Giordano assembled her design. She photocopied Kahlo's face from a book of Kahlo paintings and drew Kahlo-inspired imagery around the face. She made a photocopy transparency of her design, to use as a positive and created a photo emulsion stencil for her printing screen.

Next, using a craft knife, Giordano cut a stencil of leaves from clear contact paper. She applied the stencil directly to the shirt and used an atomizer to spray on gold fabric paint. When the leaves were dry, she screened over them with the Kahlo design, using a blend technique: she applied red, gold, and green in sequence across the screen and blended them with the squeegee, for a rainbow effect.

Peggy DeBell created this shirt, titled *Kitchen Karma*, by making a collage on paper which she took to a photo shop that offers photo transfer. She reversed the image, because it had to be transferred back onto the shirt. It was transferred with a heat process, using a large T-shirt press. DeBell took the shirt home and painted the background by brushing fabric paint onto a household sponge. She stamped the sponge repeatedly onto the shirt until it was covered in paint. She ironed the shirt to heat-set the paint. The photo transfer is permanent.

Contributing Designers

Mary Benagh is a T-shirt designer who stamps shirts in Nashville, Tennessee. Through her business, Hot Potatoes®, she sells fabric and wall stamps, as well as rubber stamp kits.

Susan Baylies is the owner of Snake and Snake Productions in Durham, North Carolina, where she produces T-shirts based on her imagination and on ancient goddess artwork.

Thom Bruni is a marbling artist who specializes in the use of the hinged or Butterfly™ comb. He lives in Delmar, New York.

Lynne Caldwell has a BA from the University of the South in Sewanee, Tennessee, and an MFA from Savannah College of Art and Design. She lives in Asheville, North Carolina, where she makes ikat weavings and teaches art to young children.

Shiila Carson of Austin, Texas, is a clothing designer who markets her batiked clothing at craft fairs.

Chris Colando is a painter and former art director at Lark Books in Asheville, North Carolina.

Maya Contento is a professional chef, who paints, writes, and potato prints. She lives in Asheville, North Carolina.

Lenore Davis is a well-known fabric artist from Newport, Kentucky, who has exhibited her work internationally and has taught for universities, craft organizations, and major craft schools. She has produced two instructional videos on textile painting.

Kristin Day is an artist who works and lives in Albany, New York. She is an apprentice marbler at CMX arts™.

Peggy DeBell has explored the possibilities of hand-painted and printed clothing for the past 13 years. She has been a member of the Southern Highland Craft Guild since 1985. She has a studio in Asheville, North Carolina.

Mary Deprez (a.k.a. "Tye Dye Mary") lives in rustic splendor in the woods around Primm Springs, Tennessee, where she makes and sells tie-dyed T-shirts.

Marilyn Forth has taught fiber arts classes at Syracuse University. Her batik paintings are featured at galleries throughout the U.S. and her work is in many private and corporate collections.

Cyndi Fox is a rubber stamp designer and fiber artist who lives in Pacific Grove, California.

JoAnn Giordano is a well-known fiber artist from Cleveland, Ohio. Her work has been widely exhibited, including at the American Craft Museum. She teaches surface design at Kent State University and the Cleveland Institute of Art.

Brenda Goelz recently earned her Bachelor of Architecture degree at Rensselaer Polytechnic Institute in Troy, New York. She is new to marbling and has done her apprenticeship with Carl Weis at CMX arts™ in Albany, New York.

Layne Goldsmith is a fiber artist from Snohomish, Washington.

Earline Hoffmann is a freelance photographer who lives in Weaverville, North Carolina, and paints shirts for her grandchildren.

Sandra Holzman is a professional artist who paints on fabric, canvas, paper, silk, furniture, and the walls. Her highly colored paintings capture sunlight and the energy of nature. Her home and studio are in the Catskill mountains of New York.

Liz Hughey, a beloved Lark designer, passed away in 2000.

Dana Irwin is a graphic artist residing in the beloved Blue Ridge Mountains of Western North Carolina with two dogs and two cats. She designed the T-shirts for her niece and nephews.

Elma Johnson teaches art and textile design at the University of North Carolina at Asheville.

Contributing Designers

Betty Kershner has been dyeing silk and other fabrics, using batik, gutta resist, hand painting, and shibori for more than 20 years. She creates wall pieces and easy-fitting, washable garments. Some garments are pieced and constructed from a palette of colors and textures; others are sewn from the dyed silk. She lives in Sewanee, Tennessee.

Amanda Kibler is a designer who lives in Atlanta, Georgia. She specializes in surface design for apparel and home furnishings, as well as paper products.

Diana Light lives and works in the beautiful Blue Ridge Mountains of North Carolina. Her home studio, like her life, is filled with glittering glass in hundreds of forms, styles, and types. After earning her BFA in painting and printmaking, she extended her expertise to etching and painting fine glass objects. She has contributed to numerous Lark books and is the coauthor of Lark's *The Weekend Crafter Etching Glass* and the author of *The Weekend Crafter Batik*.

Michelle Lipson lives in Garrett Park, Maryland, where she makes and markets prehistoric designs for her business, "Dinosaur." She is the author of *Sew a Dinosaur*.

Shelley Lowell is a painter, sculptor, illustrator, and graphic designer. She received her BFA at Pratt Institute in New York and now teaches a variety of art classes.

K. Lee Manuel is an artist who paints primarily on leather and feathers in Santa Cruz, California. Her work is included in the permanent collections of several museums, including the American Craft Museum and the Richmond Museum of Art.

Fleta Monaghan is a studio artist who teaches art to children and adults. She lives and works in Asheville, North Carolina.

Jean Wall Penland is an artist who paints and teaches in the mountains of North Carolina. She has received both Pollock-Krasner and Adolph and Esther Gottlieb Foundation grants.

Laura Petritz designs and sells tie-dye clothing and other wearables at her store, The Mystic Eye, located in Asheville, North Carolina. The T-shirt designs are a collaborative effort between Laura and her employees, dyers Anis Starr and Brent Maynor.

Timothy Putney tie-dyed and batiked T-shirts to put himself through college. When he graduated with a degree in biogenetics, he found no market for his education but a continuing demand for his shirts. He is designer/manager of Tee's Dyes in Arlington, Massachusetts.

Tracy Sanders is the owner of Harmony Batiks in Westfield, North Carolina, where she lives with her daughter, Kianna. She is a full-time batik artist.

Mimi Schleicher is a professional marbler who lives in Weaverville, North Carolina. She was a creative consultant for the book *Marbling Paper and Fabric* (Sterling, 1991).

Geoffrey Scott-Alexander is the founder and director of Glass Lake Studio, in West Sand Lake, New York. This school of expressive arts is associated with the International School of Interdisciplinary Studies.

Lisa Shelton has been marbling and participating in craft shows for years. She has also worked as a graphic designer. She is currently marbling and taking care of her daughter, Maggie, who wears a lot of marbled clothing!

Laura Sims is the proprietor of Indigo Stone in Asheville, North Carolina. She makes and markets a wide variety of paper and fabric marbled crafts, and was a creative consultant for *Marbling Paper and Fabric* (Sterling, 1991).

Allison Smith lives in Asheville, North Carolina. Her home-based business specializes in providing deluxe tourist accommodations in remote locations around the world. She's an avid crafter and designer in addition to being a full-time mother. She has created projects for numerous Lark books including *Decorating Baskets*, *Girls' World*, and *Decorating Candles*. She's the author of Lark's *The Girls' World Book of Bath & Beauty*.

Contributing Designers

Michael Smith and **Cole Cannizaro** own and operate Chaos from their production studio in Asheville, North Carolina. They are festival clothiers, specializing in silk, rayon, and cotton.

Saralyn Spradling is an artist who sends T-shirts instead of greeting cards. She lives in Asheville, North Carolina.

Annie Stromquist has received awards for her mixed-media works on paper, which have been exhibited throughout the United States and in Europe. She lives and teaches printmaking in Long Beach, California. In her spare time, she's authoring a book on screenprinting techniques for Lark Books.

Helen Suits fell in love with batik while living in Asia. Now a resident of Gainesville, Florida, she created cotton garments for years but now specializes in silk.

George Summers, Jr. is an artist who works primarily in batik. His work has been exhibited in numerous group and one-person shows on the East Coast. He has been teaching children and adults the art of batik for more than 20 years. He lives at Brickbottom, an artist community in Somerville, Massachusetts.

Susan Swanson is a Seattle artist currently working with stamping and sewn resist shibori techniques on fabric.

Lori Barraco Sylvester is a counselor at St. Anne Institute, an adjunct faculty member at Russell Sage College, and a member of the training faculty at Glass Lake Studio. She is dedicated to bringing the expressive arts into settings where rehabilitation and healing can happen. Marbling is one beautiful facet of her work. She lives in Watervliet, New York.

Scotti and **Tracey Tardiff** are screen print artists and owners of Back Porch Design, located in Sugar Grove, North Carolina. They design and market their line of T-shirts that depict the natural world and man's place within it. All their shirts are 100-percent cotton and are screened with water-based dyes.

Terry Taylor lives and works in Asheville, North Carolina, as an editor and project coordinator for Lark Books. He is a prolific designer and exhibiting artist, and works in media ranging from metals and jewelry to paper crafts and mosaics. He's also the author of numerous Lark books, including *The Artful Egg*, *Candlescaping*, and the successful series of wizard books for children.

Carl Weis is founder of CMX arts™ in Albany, New York, a not-for-profit organization dedicated to bringing the magical powers of marbling into community settings that make a difference in people's lives. He holds an MFA in painting from Columbia University and has taught studio art at the college level for more than 30 years. He is now a full-time marbler and teacher of marbling.

Marcia Winters is a freelance graphic designer who lives in Knoxville, Tennessee.

Ellen Zahorec is a mixed-media studio artist, specializing in handmade paper and collage. Her work has been shown internationally and is part of numerous private and corporate collections. She lives in Cincinnati, Ohio.

A Note About Suppliers

Usually, the supplies you need for making the projects in Lark books can be found at your local craft supply store, discount mart, home improvement center, or retail shop relevant to the topic of the book. Occasionally, however, you may need to buy materials or tools from specialty suppliers. In order to provide you with the most up-to-date information, we have created a listing of suppliers on our Website, which we update on a regular basis. Visit us at www.larkbooks.com, click on "Craft Supply Sources," and then click on the relevant topic. You will find numerous companies listed with their web address and/or mailing address and phone number.